Cambridge Elements

Elements in Politics and Communication
edited by
Stuart Soroka
University of California

SOCIAL MEDIA DEMOCRACY MIRAGE

How Social Media News Fuels a Politically Uninformed Participatory Democracy

Homero Gil de Zúñiga
University of Salamanca
Pennsylvania State University
Diego Portales University

Hugo Marcos-Marne
University of Salamanca

Manuel Goyanes
Charles III University of Madrid

Rebecca Scheffauer
University of Salamanca

Shaftesbury Road, Cambridge CB2 8EA, United Kingdom

One Liberty Plaza, 20th Floor, New York, NY 10006, USA

477 Williamstown Road, Port Melbourne, VIC 3207, Australia

314–321, 3rd Floor, Plot 3, Splendor Forum, Jasola District Centre, New Delhi – 110025, India

103 Penang Road, #05–06/07, Visioncrest Commercial, Singapore 238467

Cambridge University Press is part of Cambridge University Press & Assessment, a department of the University of Cambridge.

We share the University's mission to contribute to society through the pursuit of education, learning and research at the highest international levels of excellence.

www.cambridge.org
Information on this title: www.cambridge.org/9781009500869

DOI: 10.1017/9781009053266

© Homero Gil de Zúñiga, Hugo Marcos-Marne, Manuel Goyanes and Rebecca Scheffauer 2024

This publication is in copyright. Subject to statutory exception and to the provisions of relevant collective licensing agreements, no reproduction of any part may take place without the written permission of Cambridge University Press & Assessment.

When citing this work, please include a reference to the DOI 10.1017/9781009053266

First published 2024

A catalogue record for this publication is available from the British Library

ISBN 978-1-009-50086-9 Hardback
ISBN 978-1-009-05509-3 Paperback
ISSN 2633-9897 (online)
ISSN 2633-9889 (print)

Cambridge University Press & Assessment has no responsibility for the persistence or accuracy of URLs for external or third-party internet websites referred to in this publication and does not guarantee that any content on such websites is, or will remain, accurate or appropriate.

Social Media Democracy Mirage

How Social Media News Fuels a Politically Uninformed Participatory Democracy

Elements in Politics and Communication

DOI: 10.1017/9781009053266
First published online: November 2024

Homero Gil de Zúñiga
University of Salamanca
Pennsylvania State University
Diego Portales University
Hugo Marcos-Marne
University of Salamanca
Manuel Goyanes
Charles III University of Madrid
Rebecca Scheffauer
University of Salamanca

Author for correspondence: Homero Gil de Zúñiga, hgz@usal.es

Abstract: For over two decades, political communication research has hailed the potentially reinvigorating effect of social media on democracy. Social media was expected to provide new opportunities for people to learn about politics and public affairs, and to participate politically. Building on two systematic literature reviews on social media, and its effects on political participation and knowledge (2000–2020), and introducing empirical evidence drawing on four original US survey datasets expanding over a decade (2009–2019), this Element contends that social media has only partially fulfilled this tenet, producing a *Social Media Democracy Mirage*. That is, social media have led to a socio-political paradox in which people are more participatory than ever, yet not necessarily more informed.

Keywords: social media, political participation, political knowledge, social networking sites, systematic literature review

© Homero Gil de Zúñiga, Hugo Marcos-Marne, Manuel Goyanes and Rebecca Scheffauer 2024

ISBNs: 9781009500869 (HB), 9781009055093 (PB), 9781009053266 (OC)
ISSNs: 2633-9897 (online), 2633-9889 (print)

Contents

1 Introduction

Social science scholars have long been aware of the complexities and precarities of democratic governance, and the challenges regarding the consolidation of democratic institutions. In fact, recent years have seen increasing concerns about the state of democracy worldwide. Freedom House, a nongovernmental organization well known for its monitoring of democracy and freedom around the world, suggested in 2020 that the world had been undergoing a fifteen-year democratic decline (Gorokhovskaia et al., 2023). The Council of Europe has similarly reported that democracy is increasingly at risk, even in places well known for their democratic credentials (Birdwell et al., 2013).

Democratic backsliding is a multifaceted phenomenon, of course; but the technological developments in communication that shape societies across the world likely play a major role in both the sustainability and emergence of democracy (Weare, 2002). Our modern world has been dubbed a "network society," after all, heavily influenced by digital technologies (Castells, 2009). Since the early days of the twenty-first century, and in parallel with the popularization of information and communication technologies (ICTs), a mushrooming body of literature has examined the effects of digital technologies, especially social media, on various political outcomes (Bimber & Copeland, 2013; Gil de Zúñiga et al., 2010). And the role of digital media in our daily lives is only increasing over time. The Pew Research Center (2021), a nonpartisan fact tank based in the USA, estimated that at least 70 percent of American citizens used social media in 2021, a figure that barely reached 5 percent in 2005. This proliferation of social media has sparked debates in academic communities and beyond on the impact of social media on democracy.

The purpose of the current Element is thus to take stock of the burgeoning literature exploring associations between social media and both (1) political knowledge and (2) political participation. There is of course a longstanding literature highlighting the role of participation and knowledge in sustaining healthy democracies (e.g., Boulianne, 2020; Galston, 2001; Hopp et al., 2020; Kleinberg & Lau, 2019; Lecheler & de Vreese, 2017; Lelkes, 2020; Parry et al., 1992). But what does twenty years of research tell us about the impact of social media on these critical outcomes? Our findings, in sum, are as follows.

The existing literature suggests, in short, that social media use is associated with increased political participation (see Boulianne, 2020; Gil de Zúñiga et al., 2012; Halpern et al., 2017). For instance, studies exploring the connection between social media use and social movements suggest that the use of social media has led to a growing likelihood of engaging both in online and offline political activities. This has been found for movements such as Black Lives Matter in the USA (Cox, 2017; Mundt et al., 2018; Wilkins et al., 2019), the

15-M square-occupation movement in Spain (Micó & Casero-Ripollés, 2014), the 2011 Egypt uprising (Clarke & Kocak, 2020), student and environmental mobilization in Chile (Scherman et al., 2015), or antigovernment protest in Thailand (Sinpeng, 2021).

The story is rather different where political knowledge is concerned, however. Social media platforms were initially theorized as community spaces with the potential to contribute to a democratic public sphere and to foster political learning, whether employing intentional news-seeking or through incidental exposure to news and political discussions (Trenz, 2009; Valeriani & Vaccari, 2016). These positive expectations have not been thoroughly confirmed by empirical analyses. Indeed, recent research suggests that social media, far from having a positive effect on political knowledge, may actually prevent political learning (Cacciatore et al., 2018; Lee & Xenos, 2019; Shehata & Strömbäck, 2018). Empirical studies suggest that people either learn less as compared to those who are exposed to traditional news, or there are null direct effects derived from using social media for news (Gil de Zuñiga, Borah & Goyanes, 2021; Knobloch-Westerwick & Meng, 2011; Skovsgaard & Andersen, 2020; Valenzuela et al., 2018). In a recent meta-analysis Amsalem and Zoizner (2023) likewise raised doubt about the positive effects of social media on political knowledge. According to their results, knowledge gains are small to nonexistent. In short, there are well-founded concerns that social media use for news may not consistently contribute to a more informed public opinion.

Combining the results of these two strands of literature, political participation and political knowledge, it stands to reason that social media may be nurturing a socio-political paradox where people are increasingly more participatory, yet not necessarily more informed. In this Element, we label this phenomenon as the *Social Media Democracy Mirage* and argue that this paradox may be key to understanding many of the current political phenomena affecting liberal democracies. Specifically, the Social Media Democracy Mirage entails the amplification of political beliefs and activities on social media which are not necessarily sustained by factual information about politics. While we do not claim that the widespread use of social media will unmistakably push societies into a pathway of democratic erosion, we believe the *mirage* label resonates with the unfulfilled potential of social media use for information.

This Element includes three sections that can be read independently or as a whole:

- a systematic literature review of social media and political participation (Section 2)

- a systematic literature review of social media and political knowledge (Section 3)
- a quantitative analytical assessment of the link between social media, political knowledge, and participation using survey data from the USA (Section 4)

In the literature review Sections 2 and 3, we present an overview of the growing body of work connecting social media, political participation, and political knowledge. We examine more than 500 peer-reviewed articles which were published in over 150 journals from 2001 to 2020. Our systematic reviews contribute to the ongoing discussion on the interplay between the affordances for action that social media enables, and citizens' means to obtain information about public affairs. In Section 4 of the Element, we take advantage of a unique collection of four original datasets collected online in the USA between 2009 and 2020. Relying on these data, we further illustrate the participatory yet uninformed consequences of social media news use that underline the Social Media Democracy Mirage. Section 5 contains some concluding remarks and suggestions for future research in political communication.

Before diving into our analyses, however, the following sections (1) define political participation and knowledge, (2) describe the function and process of systematic literature reviews, and (3) outline the theoretical framework – more specifically, the "research clusters" that structure our literature reviews and empirical analysis.

1.1 Defining Participation and Knowledge

The definitions of political participation often gravitate around the identification of activities aiming at influencing policy-making or government actions (Verba et al., 1995). While many were initially associated with "offline electoral activities," such as working for a political party or voting (Conway, 1985; Saldaña et al., 2015), the emergence of the internet has broadened our conception of political participation to include, for instance, campaign contributions, protesting, writing a letter to a politician, and so on, both online and offline (Halpern et al., 2017; Yang & DeHart, 2016).

Citizens' participation is a fundamental building block for most notions of democracy (Parvin, 2018). Declines in voter turnout have thus raised concern among social science scholars, particularly considering that turnout rates may be lower than the official turnout figures, especially where there are gaps between registered voters and voting-age population. These gaps increase considerably in elections other than national ones, such as state elections, and can be found across countries and regions beyond the USA (Lijphart, 1997). Although low election turnout is often seen as a consequence of the malfunctioning of democracies

(Grönlund & Setälä, 2007), representative democracies also benefit from the electoral participation as such participation is not only the outcome of democratic illness, but also a potential means to deal with this issue. Some democratic theorists underscore that higher levels of voter turnout increase the chances that the voices of various groups in society are heard (Rosema, 2007), and this is particularly important if we consider that the chances of abstaining are not randomly distributed among the population. Young, less educated, and low-income people are consistently less likely to vote (Blais et al., 2004; Gallego, 2009; Lijphart, 1997; Wattenberg, 2020). In that sense, social media news use could be an interesting tool to foster electoral participation among young people, who are more likely to be present online (Hargittai & Hinnant, 2008), and also older people from cohorts that were early socialized in social media environments (Prensky, 2001).

Beyond voting, political participation is even more important for alternative understandings of democracy such as the deliberative one, which builds upon the exchange of ideas between individuals that do not form a homogeneous group (Steiner et al., 2017). A textbook example of the importance of participation can be seen in the design of current mechanisms for democratic innovation (e.g., participatory budgets, mini-publics, deliberative meetings, etc.), which often offer alternative spaces for citizens' engagement in political life. In this regard, we can think of political participation as an opportunity for citizens from diverse backgrounds to be treated as equals in public affairs and reduce spaces for demagogies, oppressive rules, and government inefficiencies. In sum, there is an overall agreement on the importance of participation in a democracy, and such participation can take many different forms.

Some vital forms of political participation in our empirical analysis include attending rallies and demonstrations, sending letters or emails to political organizations, newspapers, or elected officials, or volunteering to help with political causes. Although they are different, these forms of participation share a minimal core: they relate to citizens' voices being heard in the public sphere (online and analogical). Some forms of political participation associated with protest are more often used by underprivileged groups (Lipsky, 1968; van Stekelenburg & Klandermans, 2013), which show the potential of social media news use to foster types of participation not so conditioned by structural inequalities. Although some theorists call for an adjustment of our expectations on the extent to which widespread participation can be achieved (Parvin, 2018), there is little doubt that important shortcomings of liberal democracies such as the USA could be addressed with it.

Another key for democracies is political knowledge, which is broadly defined as "the various bits of information about politics that citizens hold" (Delli Carpini

& Keeter, 1993, p. 1179). Looking at the minimal representative core of democracy, voters are expected to cast their votes after considering various political alternatives, a task that can be more easily achieved when abundant political knowledge is available. In this regard, individuals who are more knowledgeable in politics are better equipped to choose parties that are in line with their preferred issues, and their positioning in these issues (Andersen et al., 2005). These knowledgeable individuals are also more likely to exercise reasoned economic voting (Gomez & Wilson, 2001) and to react to credible corruption accusations (Weitz-Shapiro & Winters, 2017). Political knowledge is closely associated with media literacy, a variable capturing the ability of individuals to engage constructively with journalism (Maksl et al., 2015) that is crucial to avoid fake news (Bulger & Davison, 2018). The relevance of the duo media literacy–political knowledge is beyond doubt in the context of electoral campaigns increasingly shaped by fake news (Allcott & Gentzkow, 2017; Mutahi & Kimari, 2020; Quandt et al., 2019; Rosa, 2019).

The positive effects of political knowledge also spread beyond the realm of elections. For example, the mechanisms of direct democracy, such as referendums, are sometimes implemented as a way to address some limitations of representative democracies, creating spaces for individuals to express their preferences without the mediation of institutions or parties. However, the ability an individual has to express their own voice often depends on political knowledge (Christin et al., 2002; Hobolt, 2007). Likewise, more knowledgeable individuals might find it easier to participate in social movements that are in line with their ideas, attitudes, and preferences, and to choose more effective ways to influence elected officials. Additionally, political knowledge correlates with the acceptance of democratic principles, which explains why some governments invest time and money to improve political knowledge among their citizens (Galston, 2001).

1.2 Systematic Literature Reviews

Despite its substantive importance, the direction and magnitude of the effects of social media on political participation and political knowledge remain unclear. Unlike other communication research domains (Ahmed et al., 2019; Garrido et al., 2011; Naab & Sehl, 2017; Wang et al., 2019; Williams, 2019), we lack a thorough and organized examination of empirical findings with a holistic narrative that is able to guide future social scientific theoretical and empirical endeavors. The purpose of our systematic literature reviews is thus to better unravel the association between social media use and both political knowledge and political participation. Our systematic reviews particularly contribute to the literature as follows.

- They examine and problematize the items and measurements used thus far in the literature focusing on political knowledge and political participation. This is particularly important because different streams of literature may have distinct definitions and measurements that complicate comparative interpretations of main findings.
- They help understand the granularity of the published material in terms of research patterns (territory of data collection, authorship structure, methodological approaches, etc.), which is key to unraveling underexplored areas and limitations.

1.3 Theoretical Framework

Before we present the literature review, we lay out our four-faceted main theoretical frameworks that underpin research on the links between social media and political participation and political knowledge. The defined facets of the theoretical framework were established in an iterative process. A priori facets were entered into conversation and dialogue with post-hoc analysis of the studies under scrutiny, yielding five potential clusters of research: (1) media effects, (2) interpersonal communication, (3) expressive political content, (4) structural effects, and (5) a miscellanea category. Figure 1 illustrates the research foci of studies situated at the intersection of social media, political participation, and political knowledge discussed in the literature reviews (Sections 2 and 3), highlighting and distinguishing the categories in which relevant papers can fall. We also point out the most salient authors for each research strand. These authors were chosen either due to their number of publications within the research clusters topics or by the impact of their findings in the literature, which we will discuss in later Sections 2 and 3. We also briefly present the theoretical foundations of each facet.

1.3.1 Media Effects

Media effects have been a research pillar in political science even before social media became relevant. Researchers have examined the effects of exposure to traditional and later to online news (Bimber & Copeland, 2013; Martin, 2008; McLeod et al., 1999). In a functioning democracy, media fulfils a variety of functions ranging from holding those in power accountable to providing citizens with the information they need to make informed decisions. With the advent of the internet, there is more information than ever before and social

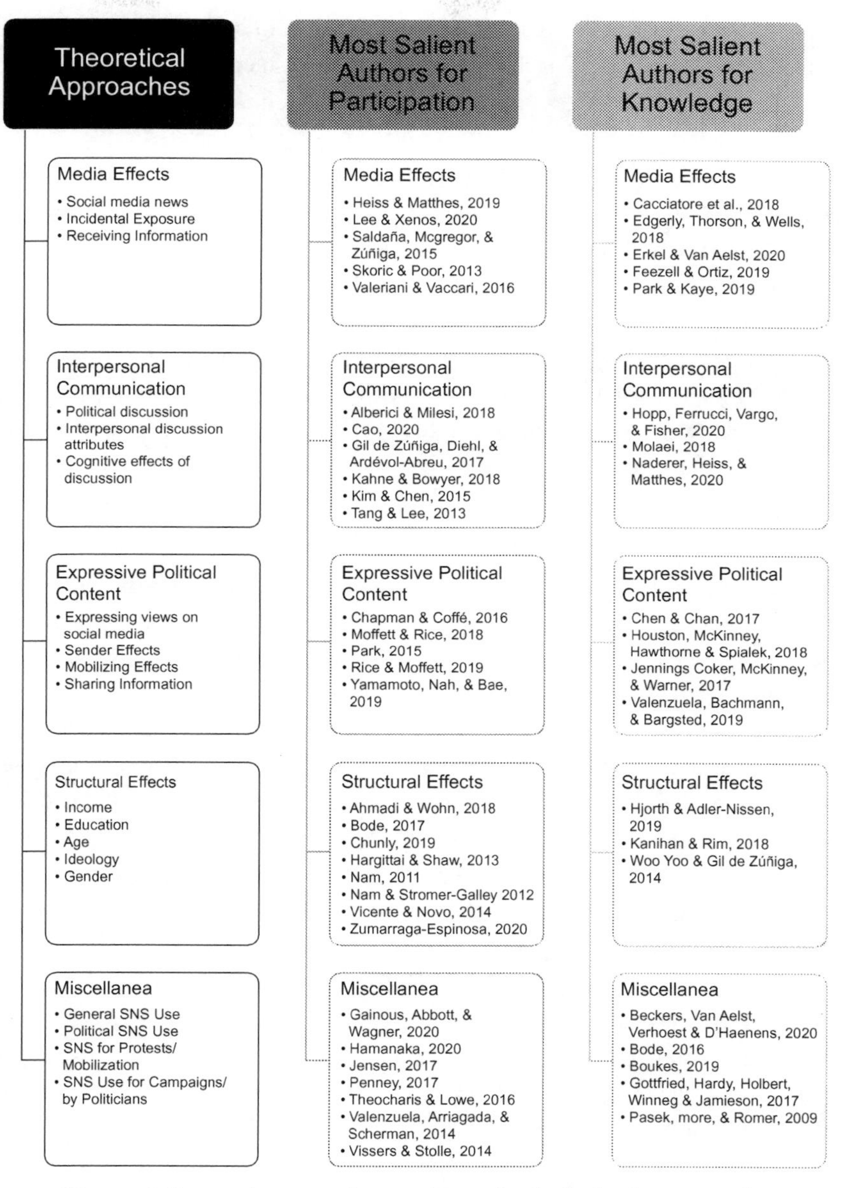

Figure 1 Research categories serving as basis for both systematic literature reviews.

media allows for easy distribution and consumption. With these developments, new research topics within media effects emerged, including the effects of social media news, second screening, and incidental news exposure (Giglietto & Selva, 2014; Heiss & Matthes, 2019; Pastrana Valls, 2017; Saldaña et al., 2015). Thus, we expect media effects on political knowledge and political participation to be as prevalent on social media as they are with traditional media.

1.3.2 Interpersonal Communication Effects

Another relevant theoretical angle to account for the relationship between social media and political participation/political knowledge is interpersonal communication. This entails studies focusing on "political discussion, the rational, deliberative exchange of arguments, and its implications for an informed and participatory citizenry" (Scheufele, 2000, p. 727). Such a form of discussion has been previously outlined as an integral antecedent for engaging in a variety of political activities (Huckfeldt & Sprague, 1995; Shah et al., 2005; Valenzuela et al., 2012) and it has even been referred to as the soul of democracy (De Tocqueville, 1863).

1.3.3 Expressive Political Content

The third research framework revolves around expressive political content or, more generally, sender or self-effects. This line of work refers to the effects that sending a message has on the sender themselves (Pingree, 2015; Shah, 2016; Valkenburg, 2017), potentially leading to a change in emotions, attitudes, cognitions, as well as behaviors (Aronson, 1999; Gil de Zúñiga et al., 2015; Pingree, 2007; Rojas & Puig-i-Abril, 2009; Valkenburg, 2017). In offline settings, attempts to persuade others also affect the potential persuader (Janis & King, 1954), which is sometimes referred to as self-persuasion (Aronson, 1999). An additional aspect associated with self-effects is the writing paradigm that has experienced newfound popularity with the internet (Ko & Kuo, 2009; Lee et al., 2016; Pennebaker, 1997), as it allows smooth political expression in the virtual realm.

The internet and social media in particular come with several affordances that can amplify self-effects in comparison to the offline realm. First of all, it allows for what Castells (2007) refers to as mass self-communication, making it possible to reach a global audience. Furthermore, users are more inclined to share information and express themselves than in an offline setting (Christofides et al., 2009). Since it allows for asynchronous communication and provides the option to easily reach a larger audience, social media lends itself as an expression hub, opening the possibility to more self-effects (Boyd, 2010; Shah, 2016).

1.3.4 Structural Effects

This cluster of research addresses the role of structural variables, mainly socioeconomic status, gender, education, internet access, and digital skills, many of which are shown to impact online and offline participation. Higher-income and socio-economic status tend to go hand in hand with better education, which in turn relates to skill and access levels. For decades, many researchers have dedicated their time and efforts to investigating the potential influences of these variables on different types of political variables. Thus, it is expected that the intersection of social media and structural variables has emerged as a popular research subject. Different theories have been proposed in this context from the "rich get richer" approach to contrary effects of the internet and social media being able to bridge gaps that are usually widened by differences in education, income, or gender. Social media is a free, fairly simple, and time-efficient tool to get engaged in politics. Thus, the fourth framework will focus on these variables.

2 Social Media and Political Participation

In gathering the articles for this task, we strictly follow the Preferred Reporting Items for Systematic reviews and Meta-Analyses (PRISMA) guidelines that transparently identify a number of criteria widely used for reporting literature reviews and meta-analyses (Moher et al., 2015). The literature search was conducted in February 2021 using academic search databases, namely Scopus, Academic Search Ultimate, and Web of Science, to compile a comprehensive review. In order to identify relevant articles, we used the following keywords: "political participation" AND "social media" OR "social networking sites and political participation" OR "Twitter and political participation" OR "Facebook and political participation." Studies (i.e., articles) included in the analysis should meet the following criteria: written in English and published by a peer-review journal (indexed in Journal of Citation Reports (JCR) and/or Scopus) between 2000 and 2021. We decided to sample this time frame because we aimed to provide the most updated literature review on the subject.

After applying the aforementioned criteria, the initial search yielded 1,348 results for social media and political participation. We then used reference management software Zotero to scan our results to find all duplicates (612 articles were removed). We carefully read the abstracts and excluded the journals that were either not peer-reviewed or off-topic before eliminating 310 articles (e.g., articles not concerned with political participation, articles focused on nonsocial media aspects such as TV news, radio, or the internet in general, research summaries, theoretical papers, or research recommendations, articles about social networks in the offline realm). We kept a total of 426 articles after applying these criteria (see Figure 2).

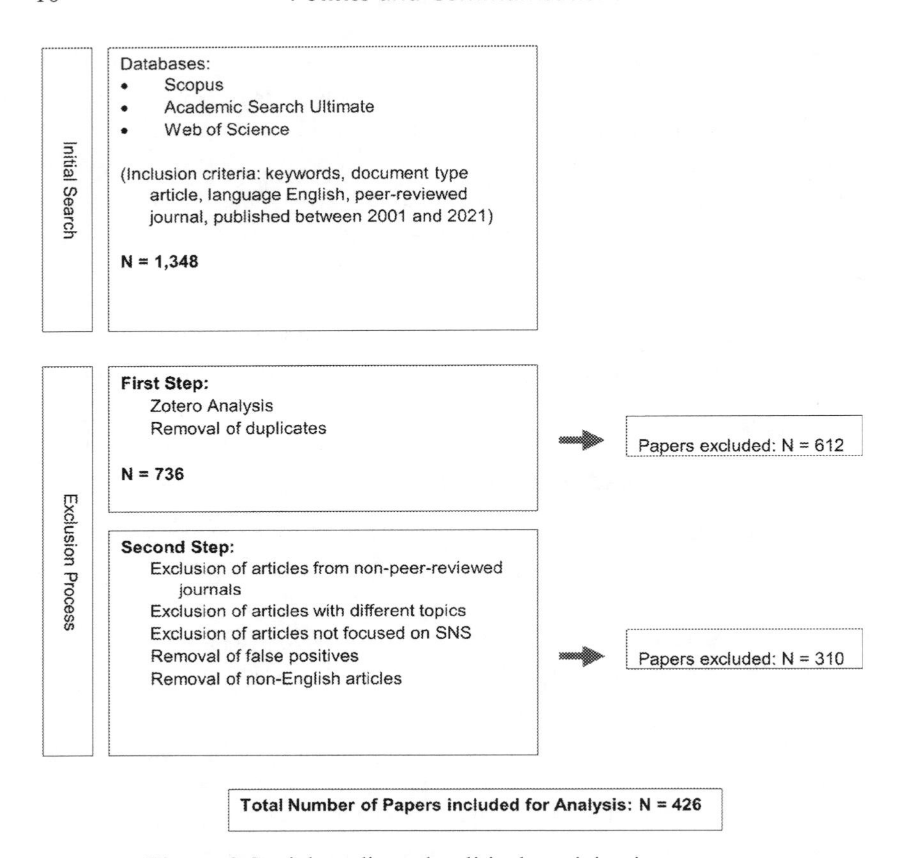

Figure 2 Social media and political participation process.

2.1 Quantitative Analysis

We started the analysis by collecting 426 articles which discuss the effects of social media on political participation. These articles were published in 176 different journals – *New Media & Society* published the largest number of articles (n = 31), followed by *Information Communication & Society* (n = 27). Seven journals altogether account for almost one third of all published articles (n = 135), while 105 journals only published one article each. A full list of the journals can be found in Table 1A.

Regarding authorship, USA-based scholars led research efforts in the sub-field with 137 publications, followed by scholars based in the UK (n = 30), Hong Kong (n = 21), Australia (n = 17), and Canada (n = 17). As for the country of data collection, a large majority of the papers used data from the USA (n = 117), followed by China (n = 19), the UK (n = 18), and South Korea (n = 15). While there are 65 different countries represented in the analytical framework, only 46 articles are comparative in nature. Articles on social media and political participation started to emerge in 2001, but research in this domain skyrocketed after 2011 and peaked in 2020 with 109 publications.

For the measurement of social media use, most of the studies utilized overall social media indicators or inquired about different platforms that were later combined into one averaged index (n = 298). For distinct measurements, Facebook was consistently selected as the most representative social media platform to be studied (n = 68), followed by Twitter (n = 38). There are, however, several studies focusing on other social media platforms, partially unique to certain geographic areas, such as Weibo in China or VK in Russia (n = 16). An overview over the items used most commonly for measurements can be found in Tables 4A–14A.

In terms of methods, 317 articles drew upon quantitative data, while 68 used qualitative methods and 39 combined quantitative and qualitative methodological approaches. Most quantitative studies relied on survey data (n = 241), content analysis (n = 58), and mixed methods (n = 52). A total of 20 studies used interviews and 10 others employed focus groups. Moreover, 14 studies followed experimental designs and nine relied on ethnography and participant observation. The remaining 22 articles were grouped under "other" methodologies (e.g., case studies, or principal component analyses).

Most papers (n = 345) focused on citizens as a primary unit of analysis, while some articles addressed political leaders (n = 21) and democratic systems as a whole (n = 6) and others concentrated on more than one of the aforementioned units (e.g., leaders and citizens) (n = 20). Of the articles, 33 included video clips, websites, or songs as units of the analysis or main object of investigation. A large majority of the papers (n = 366) relied on cross-sectional data, while 38 articles used longitudinal data and 15 articles combined both. For the remaining 7 articles, neither one of those descriptions was applicable, as they were mostly theoretical. The summary of the data can be seen in the following graphs (Figures 3 to 5 and Figure 1A). More detailed information on the data used in the figures can be found in Tables 2A and 3A.

2.2 Qualitative Analysis: Thematic Patterns of Social Media and Political Participation Research

2.2.1 Main Findings

In general, it appears that the use of social media news to some degree replicates the influence that the use of traditional news exerts on political participation. Despite few studies presenting contrary results, deliberate use of news on social networking sites, regardless of the social media platform or specific

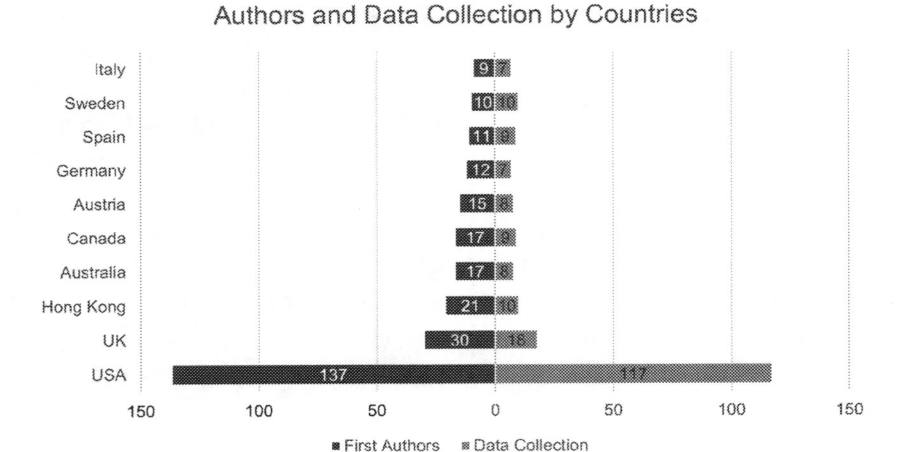

Figure 3 Data collection and first author origins depicted by country.

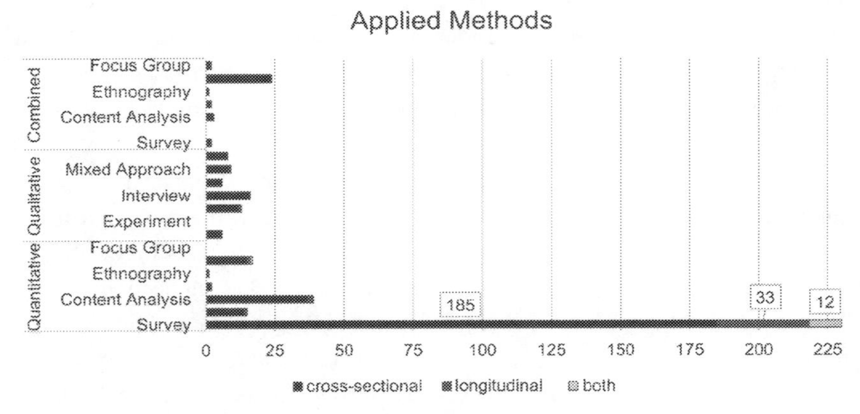

Figure 4 Number of studies depicted by applied methods, additionally divided by quantitative or qualitative as well as cross-sectional, longitudinal, and combined data collection.

measurement, positively relates to participation. Incidental exposure, on the other hand, is more complex to pin down and only has positive effects under certain conditions. In terms of interpersonal communication, network size and discussion seem to produce the most consistent effects on participation. For expression, pinning down effects is somewhat more complex as studies tend to fold expressive behaviors into other social media measurements. Finally, in terms of structural effects researchers point to a still existent gender gap with men engaging in more visible participatory behaviors. For younger people, social media plays a bigger part when it comes to engagement which is often

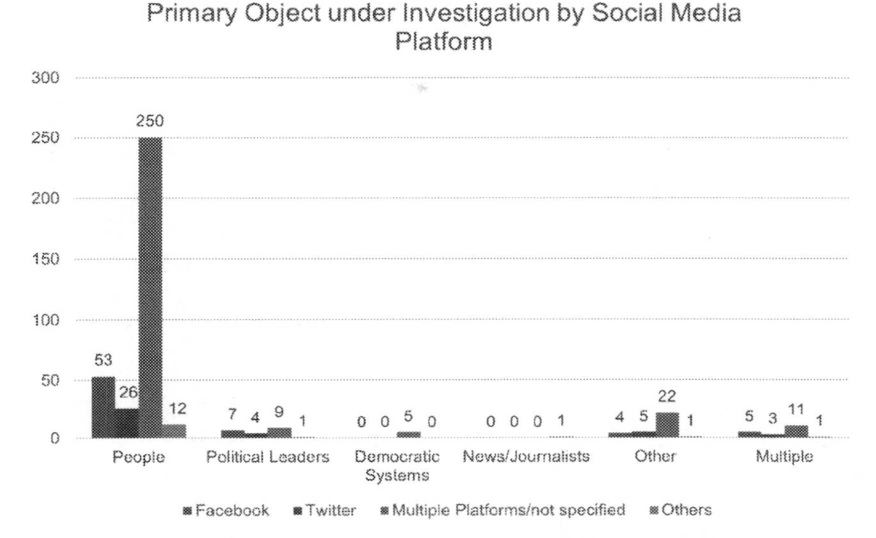

Figure 5 Number of studies depicted by the primary objects under investigation, additionally divided by social media platform in question.

noted as a positive trend. The expectation that social media might help previously disadvantaged groups (those with less income and/or less education) has been mostly disproved.

2.2.2 Measuring Political Participation

A challenge for the comparability of the results has to do with the diverse ways in which political participation is measured. Most researchers measure both online and/or offline participation with different political activities and a different number of items (Ahmed & Cho, 2019; Park & Kaye, 2018; Saldaña et al., 2015; Stromback et al., 2018; Towner & Muñoz, 2018). Some scholars, however, focus more on participation measures capturing aspects such as voting (Diehl et al., 2019; Towner, 2013), activism/protest (Diehl et al., 2019; Karakaya & Glazier, 2019), or low- and high-effort participation (Heiss & Matthes, 2019). Despite these different approaches, a vast majority of the studies showcased a positive influence of social media use on political participation.

2.2.3 Media Effects

Despite the extensive research conducted so far, the magnitude of the associations between media and political participation remains uncertain (Ahmad et al., 2019; Li et al., 2016; Saldaña et al., 2015). Based on the positive influence traditional media use was found to have, many expected news consumption on social media to similarly impact participatory behaviors. Saldaña and colleagues (2015), for instance, presented results from the UK and the USA that attest to the significant impact of media (e.g., traditional news and social media news, the latter of which was captured with eight items) in predicting online and offline political participation. The mobilizing impact of social media is replicated in other countries (Skoric & Poor, 2013; Stromback et al., 2018; Zhang & Lin, 2014) where media variables, such as informational social media use (six items), social media news use (three items), and the interaction of Facebook use and attention to traditional news, were applied. In most studies, social media news consumption appears to positively influence political participation online and offline (Gil de Zúñiga et al., 2014; Park & Kaye, 2018; Saldaña et al., 2015).

Beyond intentional exposure to news in social media, both survey-based studies and experimental studies have focused on the impact of incidental news exposure (Heiss & Matthes, 2019, 2021; Lee & Xenos, 2020; Lu, 2019). Some researchers voiced the hope that incidental exposure to news might be able to produce similar results to deliberate news consumption and could, thus, bridge the gap between those who are already engaged in politics and those who are largely uninterested. Experimental approaches have evidenced that encountering political information embedded in a humorous context can increase the likelihood of political participation – directly and indirectly via elaboration, which might be more marked for those who generally would not engage with political information on social media (Heiss & Matthes, 2021). Lee and Xenos (2020) highlighted that the relationship between incidental news exposure and political participation is reciprocal, influencing each other indirectly via political social media use. Moreover, results from a two-wave panel study suggested that the potential influence of incidental news exposure depends strongly on how participation is measured. While there is a direct positive influence on low-effort online participation, the effect on high-effort online participation is conditional on political interest (Heiss & Matthes, 2019).

Another viable research avenue within media effects that has recently garnered attention is the effect of second or dual screening. Users actively search for more information on or discuss about, for example, candidates while watching a debate, thereby engaging with more information and, as was theorized, might then be more inclined to engage in politics themselves. Vaccari and Valeriani (2018b), for example, showed that dual screening for political content positively influences online and offline political participation and additionally interacts with political interest. Results from twenty different countries further validated those findings, showing a positive association between second screening and political participation and even political expression on social media (Gil de Zúñiga & Liu, 2017). Lin (2019) found similar tendencies for civic engagement and highlighted that dual screening leads to higher civic engagement attitudes, which in turn fosters engagement. In addition to these positive indications stemming from survey research, Giglietto and Selva (2014) used content analysis to validate the influence of second screening. Their results showed that second screening elicits political participation, specifically during interviews and group discussion programs.

In line with the importance of considering how social media use is measured, results from a three-wave panel study on campaign information showed that YouTube and Tumblr had no significant influence on any form of participation, thereby showing that platform-specific affordances can greatly impact how social media use relates to political participation. In contrast, Facebook use positively predicted online participation, while Twitter and Google+ use correlated positively with both online and offline participation. However, none of them influenced voting turnout (Towner, 2013). Nevertheless, Zhang et al. (2013) found that relying on Facebook/Google+, Twitter, and YouTube for political information positively predicted online and offline participation. Additionally, it appears that, especially for "Boomers," attention to social media is only relevant for online participation. While news use on Facebook, YouTube, or Twitter did not significantly influence the applied index of offline participation (five items), news use on Facebook and YouTube positively related to online participation (index with eight items).

Overall, several studies found a positive effect of social media (news) use on political persuasion (Kasadha, 2019), interest (Zhang et al., 2013), protest (Diehl et al., 2019; Karakaya & Glazier, 2019; Zumarraga-Espinosa, 2020), voting (Diehl et al., 2019; Hassim et al., 2020; Towner, 2013), civic engagement (Gil de Zúñiga, 2012; Kim & Chen, 2015), and environmental activism (Zhang & Skoric, 2018).

2.2.4 Interpersonal Communication

Literature on interpersonal communication in our analysis suggests that the structure of interactions on social media may be the defining feature of the effects on political behaviors. Thus, this research cluster refers to the impact of different forms of political discussion (e.g., discussion with homogeneous vs. heterogeneous networks, weak vs. strong ties), interpersonal discussion attributes (e.g., network size), and places of discussion (e.g., via mobile phones). More importantly, interpersonal communication frameworks are often combined with those of media effects because news consumption helps promote discussions (Shah et al., 2005) and broaden informational horizons that give people access to a more varied set of news (Gil de Zúñiga & Valenzuela, 2011).

Akin to media effects and political participation, academic discussions have increasingly revolved around the relations taking place on online platforms. This new space for discussion comes with several affordances that differ substantially from offline exchanges (Valenzuela et al., 2012). While offline interactions give visual cues and are synchronous as well as oral in nature, online forms of discussion can be asynchronous, written, and oftentimes anonymous (Lin, 2009). Moreover, it becomes easier to connect with a wider array of people online, potentially boosting people's network size and the number of weak-tie contacts (Papacharissi, 2004), both of which are influential when it comes to promoting political participation (Granovetter, 1973; Valenzuela et al., 2012) as people are exposed to not only more information but also to more diverse content. Furthermore, whereas some scholars question the deliberative potential of online discussions (Strandberg, 2008), others underline that active online discussions may carry a positive impact on political participation, whether using formal or informal interactions. Thus, both discussions with other users and with political actors could be beneficial in boosting individuals' political participation (Abdulla et al., 2018; Akkor, 2017; Vaccari & Valeriani, 2018a).

Alberici and Milesi (2018) highlighted that it is the type of discussion that plays an integral part in encouraging participatory behaviors, urging researchers to further investigate disparate political discussion attributes. According to their results, it is specifically constructive online discussions that can imbue a person's politicized identity with "meaning of responding to a moral obligation" (Alberici & Milesi, 2018, p. 143), making them participate in collective action online and offline. The size of people's discussion networks may also be an important contributor to online and offline participation. There appears to be a direct positive influence of network size on participation (Cao, 2020), a cross-sectional finding that was replicated by two-wave panel studies as well (Gil de Zúñiga, Diehl, et al., 2017; Gil de Zúñiga et al., 2014).

Additionally, Tang and Lee (2013) found evidence of bigger network size increasing time spent on social media sites like Facebook, which leads to exposure to more information and results in higher levels of participation. Kahne and Bowyer (2018) found that while network size and friendship-driven activities positively predict offline participation, the interaction of network size and interest-driven online activities influence online and offline participation, suggesting that more complex relationships are to be entangled by future research. Political discussion effects were found to hold true irrespective of whether researchers consider people's online or offline networks, thus underlining this as an important factor in influencing their participation (Cao, 2020; Gil de Zúñiga, Diehl, et al., 2017; Gil de Zúñiga, Molyneux, et al., 2014; Kahne & Bowyer, 2018; Tang & Lee, 2013).

Beyond the nature of exchanges and the size of networks, research has shown that cultivating heterogeneous networks sparks higher levels of political participation and even civic engagement (Kim & Chen, 2015; Tang & Lee, 2013;

Yoo & Gil de Zúñiga, 2019), an effect that was not reproduced for discussion with more homogeneous networks (Yoo & Gil de Zúñiga, 2019), once more building on the idea that these types of networks will provide more varied information which then could lead to more participation. While Tang and Lee (2013) only found a significant connection of network heterogeneity with offline participation, results presented by Yoo and Gil de Zúñiga (2019) showed that incidental news exposure influenced discussion heterogeneity, which positively affected online and offline participation. Some researchers focus their measurements of network heterogeneity specifically on with whom people discuss (Kim & Chen, 2015; Yoo & Gil de Zúñiga, 2019), whereas others consider the make-up of a person's (online) networks as a whole (Tang & Lee, 2013).

Finally, the specific place in which people get informed may also be an influential factor. Discussing politics via mobile phones (which is influenced by consuming news via smartphones), for example, positively affects offline participation (Kim et al., 2016). Even WhatsApp discussion appears to be influential, positively correlating with activism and conventional participation. These effects appear to be more pronounced for younger people (Gil de Zúñiga et al., 2019). Moreover, information-seeking seems to spur online and offline discussion. Results presented by Li and Chan (2017) show that online discussion sparks higher levels of online participation, but offline discussion influenced both online and offline participation. These findings were consistent for both Hong Kong and China. Zhang et al. (2010) also came to similar conclusions, highlighting that offline discussion positively relates to political and civic participation.

2.2.5 Expressive Political Content

Some researchers see expressive political content as a form of participation in itself (Chapman & Coffé, 2016), while others see a clear pathway from expressive content to some forms of online and offline participation (Moffett & Rice, 2018; Rice & Moffett, 2019), and even as a form of influencing and persuading other citizens (Hosch-Dayican et al., 2016; Penney, 2016). Nevertheless, building on the idea of self-effects, many expected political expression to potentially lead to more participation in the person who expressed themselves in the first place.

With expressive content, measures become more convoluted than with previously described research strands. A few studies feature separate variables dedicated solely to expressive content. Instead, many researchers chose to include this as an aspect of variables such as social media use (Robles et al., 2015; Vissers & Stolle, 2014b; Zhang & Skoric, 2018). The studies focusing on expressive actions present variables such as political expression on Snapchat (Rice & Moffett, 2019), social media prosumption (Yamamoto et al., 2019), creative internet use (Ekström & Östman, 2015), political tweeting (Bode & Dalrymple, 2016), or simply political expression on social media (Chan et al., 2017; Gil de Zúñiga, Molyneux, et al., 2014; Kwak et al., 2018).

While expressive use of social media generally appears to be an important predictor of online (Chan et al., 2017; Gil de Zúñiga et al., 2014; Yamamoto et al., 2019) and offline participation (Gil de Zúñiga et al., 2014; Kwak et al., 2018; Lane et al., 2017), some studies also highlight the importance of distinct platforms. Using Facebook or Twitter to politically express oneself has also shown a positive impact on different forms of participation (Bode & Dalrymple, 2016; Vissers & Stolle, 2014a). The influence of political expression as part of using social media and the internet also extends to positively impacting environmental activism and consumerism (Zhang & Skoric, 2018).

Furthermore, some researchers point out more intricate paths to participation. Lane et al. (2017) showed that cross-cutting discussion is what can spark information sharing on social media, which leads to online and then offline participation. Chen et al. (2017) highlighted the path from mobile news to mobile political messaging and to political expression on social media, which leads to both online and offline participation. Additionally, Yamamoto et al. (2019) introduced the concept of social media *prosumption*, which includes consuming and producing content online. Social Media prosumption will trigger more political information seeking online, more online discussion heterogeneity, and via those two, more online political participation.

2.2.6 Structural Effects

Among the structural factors influencing participation, gender is highly discussed in previous research. The affordances offered by the internet and social media seem to facilitate engagement to a bigger degree for men than for women. Vochocová et al. (2016) question the "narrowing gender gap" that is often associated with the online environment, heralding equal space and opportunities for all genders to participate. Some studies suggest that this gap is not closing, as males are more likely to participate in online political activities such as political engagement, for example, being involved political groups or charities, (Xenos et al., 2014), getting political information online (Hargittai & Shaw, 2013), sharing political opinions online (Vicente & Novo, 2014), and mobilization online (Moraes et al., 2020; Nam & Stromer-Galley, 2012). Additionally, men usually engage in behaviors that are more outgoing and visible like sharing their opinion or engaging politically online (Vicente &

Novo, 2014; Xenos et al., 2014). Despite these variations in the measurement of the dependent variables, there is consistent evidence suggesting that males are more prone to be involved in political activities online. The reasons why gender gaps appear persistent are typically due to socio-economic factors. Many forms of participation call for resources, like money and time, which might not be available to women to the same extent (Schlozman et al., 1999).

Besides gender, one of the main structural predictors of online engagement and political participation is age. Various studies have found that younger individuals are more active within the context of social media. Although the outcome variables and their measurements differ between studies (e.g., online and offline participation, liking and sharing political content online, political social media use, and mobilization), the effect appears to hold consistently for political use of social media (Bode, 2017; Nam, 2011) and for using social media information tools (Nam & Stromer-Galley, 2012). Similar results concerning age were found across countries such as Cambodia (Chunly, 2019), Finland (Strandberg, 2014), Germany (Hoffmann & Lutz, 2019), and the USA (Bode, 2017).

Education is also considered a structural influence often associated with political participation. A host of studies showed that people with higher levels of education are more likely to engage politically (Rosenstone & Wolfinger, 1980; Schlozman et al., 2013; Verba et al., 1995), as citizen's educational and internet skill levels influence the abilities to navigate on the internet and partake in political activities ; Nam, 2011). This could also be attributed to higher levels of income usually associated with those with higher education (Manski, 1992). Results regarding online activities, however, tend to be somewhat mixed. While some studies found a connection between higher education, social media use, and political activities (Ahmed & Cho, 2019; Hoffmann & Lutz, 2019; Woo Yoo & Gil de Zúñiga, 2014), others have reverse findings, pointing out positive connections of social media and participation for those with lower education (Hoffman, 2012; Nam, 2011). Bode (2017) highlighted varying effects of education depending on the type of political social media use (e.g., comments, likes, replies). This suggests that the effect of education may be contingent on a host of individual-level, meso-level, and macro-level variables.

Finally, several studies highlight the influence of income. So far, some studies follow the "rich get richer" approach and claim that financially privileged population layers in society will tend to be more politically engaged (Buente, 2015), as these citizens may have more money, time, and civic skills to partake in political activities (Brady et al., 1995). However, other scholars suggest that those who were previously excluded from the political system due to economic reasons now have more opportunities to participate online (Spaiser, 2012), as this environment calls for fewer resources in terms of time and (digital) access. Despite this, scholarship examining political inequalities related to digital connectivity argues that citizens from lower socio-economic backgrounds might often remain excluded from political activities online (Sylvester & McGlynn, 2010; Weber et al., 2003; Xu et al., 2018). While some found a positive effect of higher income on offline participation (Garcia-Castañon et al., 2011) and online participation (Bode & Dalrymple, 2016; Chunly, 2019; Hoffman, 2012; Steinberg, 2015), only a few studies produced conflicting results and show that social media help those from lower socio-economic backgrounds to be more involved (Vicente & Novo, 2014; Wang et al., 2018; Zumarraga-Espinosa, 2020).

2.2.7 Miscellanea

A number of journal articles do not easily fit into one of the four categories outlined at the beginning of Section 2. This section groups these findings together, as follows.

Overall Internet/Social Media Use. Several authors focused on social media use per se, without looking at any specific factors like news use or expressive content. While Theocharis and Lowe (2016) pointed out the negative effect of general Facebook use on traditional civic offline and online participation in Greece, other researchers highlight more positive influences. Zhang and Skoric (2018) conducted a study in Hong Kong that revealed the negative influences of relational social media use on environmental activism but pointed to positive results for environmental consumerism. Similar results for general social media use and political consumerism were found in the USA, where Gil de Zúñiga, Copeland, et al. (2014) highlighted the mediating effect of general social media use on the relationship between digital media use and political consumerism. The same study also showed a positive connection between general social media use and offline political participation. Results from all over the world seemingly corroborate this positive influence. In Iran, Da Silva Nogueira and Papageorgiou (2020) found evidence for a positive connection between social media use and online political participation, as well as online political information seeking. Mustapha and Omar (2020) confirmed these findings regarding online political participation and generic social media use in Nigeria. However, neither one of those two studies found significant results for general social media use and offline political participation. While Lee et al. (2018) also found a positive influence of social media use on political engagement in South Korea, they mentioned that these higher levels of engagement lead to more polarization.

Political Social Networking Site (SNS) Use. Many researchers specifically looked into political use of social media which includes behaviors such as reading political news, expressing political opinions, participating in online polls, or joining online causes and groups (Choi & Kwon, 2019; Valenzuela, 2013). However, although these behaviors fit into the aforementioned categories (e.g., reading political news would fall under 2.2.3 Media Effects), they are often combined into a single instrument, thus generating this new subcategory. Many studies highlight the positive influence of this type of social media use on other kinds of online and offline participation, activism, and political protest (Choi & Kwon, 2019; Chon & Park, 2020; Gainous et al., 2020; Valenzuela, 2013; Vissers & Stolle, 2014a).

Mobilizing, Protest. In addition to the political use of social media, some studies also present social media as a tool for organizing and participating in protests, as well as mobilizing people. Studies demonstrate a positive influence when applying overall social media measures (Bond et al., 2012; Costanza-Chock, 2012; Dey, 2020; Hamanaka, 2020; Joia & Soares, 2018; Maher & Earl, 2019) and hold true even for the effects showcased by distinct platforms such as Twitter, Facebook, or WhatsApp (Soares et al., 2021; Valenzuela et al., 2014). Results from several papers show the possibilities offered by social media to create a form of digital governance that includes citizens in government decision-making (Joia & Soares, 2018; Soares et al., 2021). Social media is particularly useful to organize protests and initiate mobilizations as it is used more by the vanguards of demonstrations and during times when protests are not already running high (Hamanaka, 2020; Valenzuela et al., 2014). According to Bond et al. (2012), mobilizing messages on social media does not only influence participation but also self-expression, information seeking, and voting as such mobilization can indirectly influence friends of people initially exposed to them.

SNS Use by Politicians, Legislative Bodies, and Campaigns. Several studies also investigate the adoption of SNS as a communication tool for politicians, political campaigns, political parties, as well as government bodies and institutions. Results thus far attest to the great potential and a steady rise in the implementation of SNS as a valuable political communication tool. This was documented by studies with diverse geographical backgrounds such as the USA, the UK, Sweden, and Germany (Cogburn & Espinoza-Vasquez, 2011; Gerl et al., 2018; Housholder & LaMarre, 2013; Jiang, 2017; Penney, 2017; Ridge-Newman, 2020). Other studies/scholars also found a positive influence of social media use for campaigns and politicians for either influencing participation, individual engagement, or political news consumption (e.g., Cogburn & Espinoza-Vasquez, 2011; Housholder & LaMarre, 2013), even if these effects are at times only marginal (Jensen, 2017; Larsson, 2020). These effects remained consistent across different SNS platform measures such as general SNS use, Facebook, or Twitter use (Amaral et al., 2016; Jensen, 2017; Larsson, 2020). This shows the mobilizing potential of social media. However, more research needs to be conducted as several studies highlight that politicians and legislative bodies struggle to realize the full potential of social media as communicative tools (Amaral et al., 2016; Faria & Rehbein, 2016; Pillay, 2019).

3 Social Media and Political Knowledge

This section presents findings from a systematic analysis of the relationship between social media and political knowledge. Mimicking the structure used in the preceding section, we followed the PRISMA guidelines (Moher et al., 2015) for the literature review, which was conducted in February 2021 using the following databases: Scopus, Academic Search Ultimate, and Web of Science. The following keywords were used to identify relevant articles: "political knowledge" AND "social media" OR "social networking sites and political knowledge" OR "Twitter and political knowledge" OR "Facebook and political knowledge." We included articles written in English and published in a peer-reviewed journal (indexed in JCR and/or Scopus) between 2000 and 2021.

The initial search yielded 1,556 results for social media and political knowledge. We then used Zotero to remove duplicates (808 articles) and excluded either non-peer-reviewed, off-topics, or non-English articles (673 articles). Our final sample was 75 articles (see Figure 6).

3.1 Quantitative Analysis

For this analysis, we started with a systematic search for articles relating to political knowledge and social media. After compiling a corpus of published manuscripts, we coded and sorted the articles. We began with a quantitative analysis of the articles before looking into the findings by using a qualitative analysis. The seventy-five articles on the relationship between social media and political knowledge were published in forty different journals. *New Media & Society* has the highest number of articles (n = 6), followed by the *Journal of Information Technology & Politics* (n = 5). Twenty-three journals published one article each. A majority of the first authors were based in the USA (n = 38), followed by Austria (n = 6), Hong Kong (n = 4), and the Netherlands (n = 3). Most articles used data gathered in the USA (n = 37), followed by those focusing on China, Sweden, and South Korea (n = 3). Overall, the articles analyzed data from

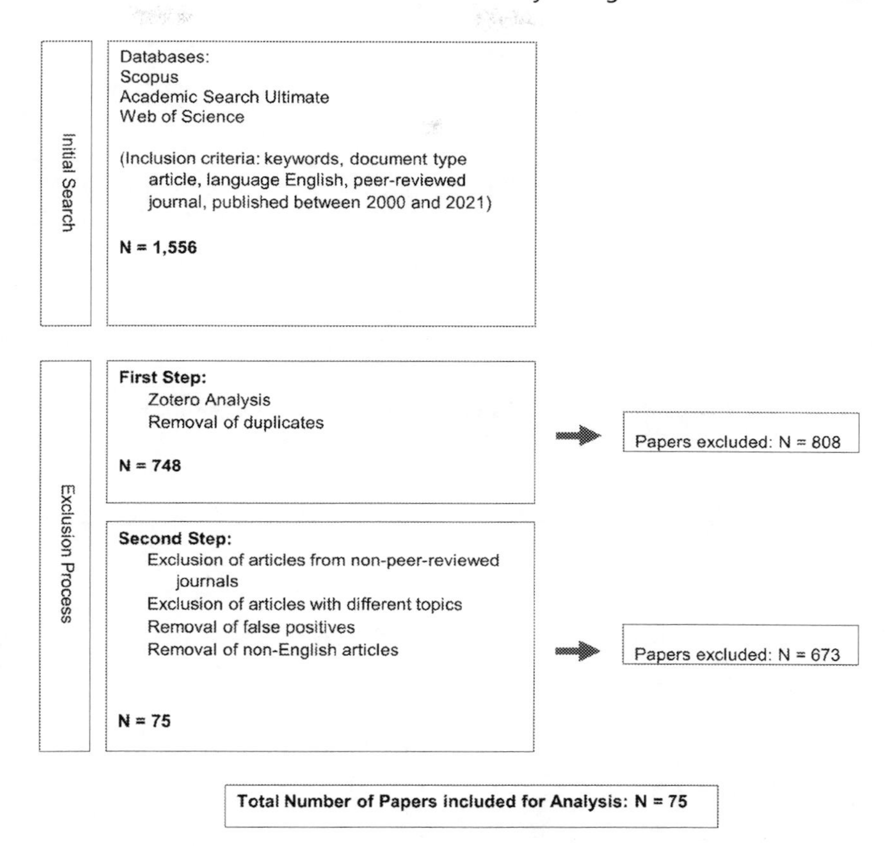

Figure 6 Social media and political knowledge process.

twenty-six countries, and three of them applied a comparative logic and included data from more than one country.

Focusing on time trends, while the first articles on political knowledge and social media were published in 2009, it was not until 2016 that the number of publications increased substantially (reaching sixteen articles published in 2020). Regarding the operationalization of social media use, most researchers either applied a general measure of social media or inquired about different platforms to combine them into one averaged measurement (n = 55). Facebook was the most popular platform for researchers (n = 12), followed by Twitter (n = 5), while some studies focused on other platforms such as Weibo or VK (n = 3). The most common items used for measuring constructs can be found in Tables 18A to 22A.

Regarding methods, seventy-two of the articles drew upon quantitative data, which evidences a clear pattern in the subfield. Two articles used qualitative methods, while one article combined quantitative and qualitative techniques. Most quantitative studies relied on survey data (n = 58), followed by

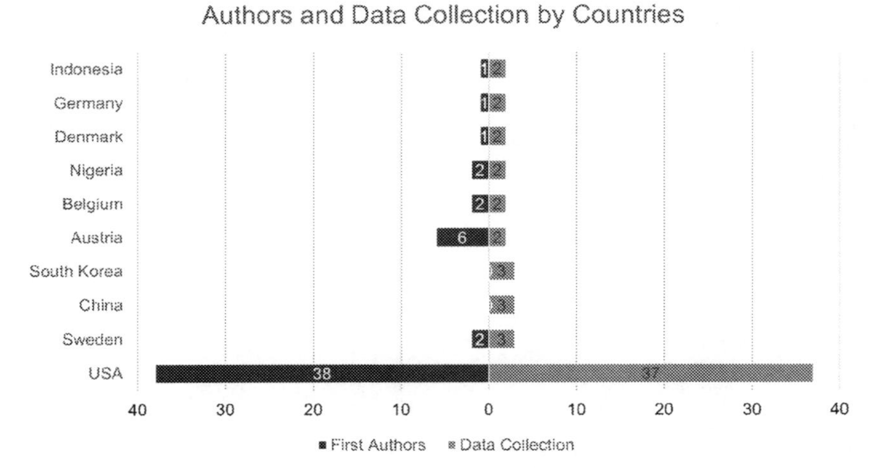

Figure 7 Data collection and first author's origins depicted by country.

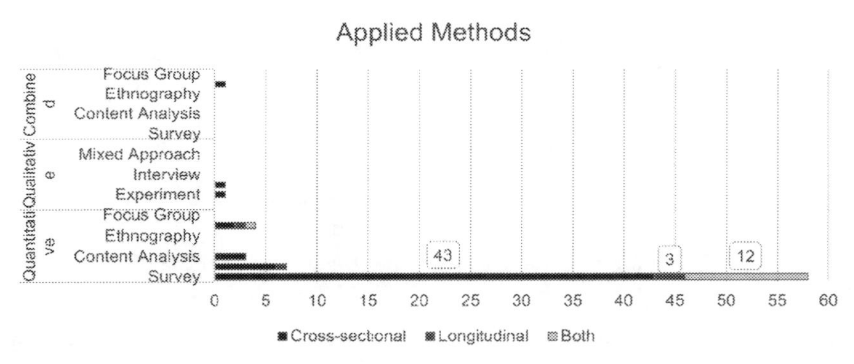

Figure 8 Number of studies depicted by applied methods, additionally divided by quantitative or qualitative methods, as well as cross-sectional, longitudinal, and combined data collection.

experiments (n = 8), mixed methods (n = 5), and content analysis (n = 4). Most papers (seventy-three) examined the relationship between social media use and political knowledge using samples of citizens, while some focused on subsamples such as students or young people. Additionally, fifty-seven articles utilized cross-sectional data, five used longitudinal data, and thirteen combined both. The quantitative results of this systematic literature review are presented in the following figures (Figures 7 to 9 and Figure 6A in the Appendix). Detailed information on the data used in these figures can be found in Tables 15A to 17A.

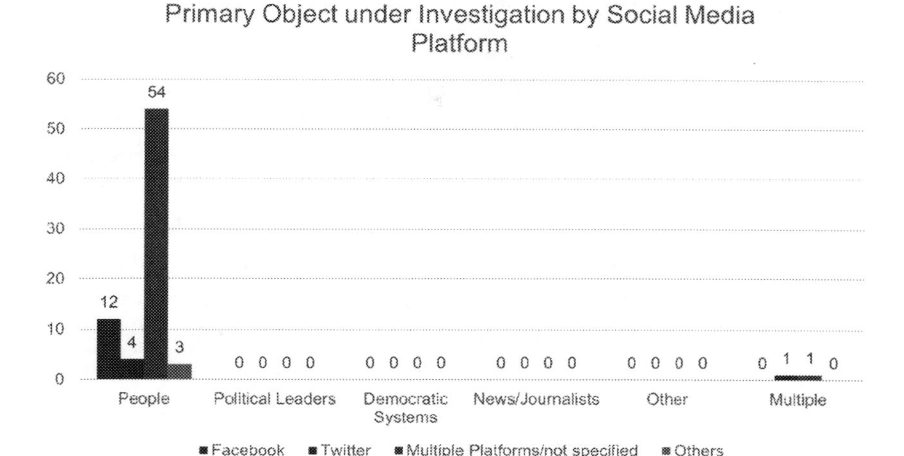

Figure 9 Number of studies depicted by the primary objects under investigation, additionally divided by social media platform in question.

3.2 Qualitative Analysis: Research Objects and Methods in Social Media and Political Knowledge Research

3.2.1 Main Findings

The biggest takeaway from the studies focused on political knowledge is that there is no agreement on effects regarding directionality, size, or whether there are any effects at all. Social media news use appears to not be influential overall, with studies showing positive, negative, and null results. Interpersonal communication was mostly only found to impact political knowledge if researchers focused on Facebook in particular (discussion and network heterogeneity), but even here the effect seemed conditional on other variables. As for expressive behavior, positive effects on knowledge can be found once said behavior is connected to cognitive elaboration. While traditional education or income are often referenced as influential factors for political knowledge, when it comes to interactions of structural variables and social media, it is ideology that produces the most consistent results.

3.2.2 Measuring Political Knowledge

The measurements for political knowledge vary across studies as the questions used need to be adapted for different countries (e.g., who the leader is, or how certain democratic processes work), including among others: Iran (Alam et al., 2019), Indonesia (Astuti & Hangsing, 2018), Denmark (Ohme, 2020), the

Philippines (David et al., 2019), China (Chen & Chan, 2017), and the USA (Beam et al., 2016; Cacciatore et al., 2018; Feezell & Ortiz, 2019). While many researchers employed the measurements of political knowledge based on the works of Delli Carpini and Keeter (1993, 1996), others created variables for specific types of political knowledge such as factual knowledge (Beam et al., 2016; Lee, 2020), campaign-related knowledge (Ohme, 2020), general-surveillance political knowledge (Edgerly et al., 2018; Erkel & Van Aelst, 2020), or general and issue-specific knowledge (Feezell & Ortiz, 2019; Woo Yoo & Gil de Zúñiga, 2014). The operationalizations of political knowledge are quite similar to those of social media studies, varying in the number of items and relying on previous concepts used by Delli Carpini & Keeter (1996) (Cacciatore et al., 2018) or Pew Research Center (Cacciatore et al., 2018; Hopp et al., 2020).

3.2.3 Media Effects

The discussion of the effects of social media on political knowledge is far from settled, despite the general agreement that traditional news use boosts political knowledge and hopes for social media replicating this influence. While some studies highlighted a positive influence of social media news use on knowledge (Alam et al., 2019; Astuti & Hangsing, 2018; Beam et al., 2016; David et al., 2019; Mwonzora, 2020; Ohme, 2020; Park & Kaye, 2019), many have found negative associations (Cacciatore et al., 2018; Chen & Chan, 2017; Erkel & Van Aelst, 2020; Gil de Zúñiga, Weeks, et al., 2017; Heiss & Matthes, 2021; Lee, 2020) or nonsignificant results (Edgerly et al., 2018; Feezell & Ortiz, 2019; Gil de Zúñiga & Diehl, 2019; Hao et al., 2014; Naderer et al., 2020; Wolfsfeld et al., 2016; Woo Yoo & Gil de Zúñiga, 2014).

As for the effects revolving around other media variables, these are quite similar and include online news reading (Beam et al., 2016), social media news use (Cacciatore et al., 2018; Chen & Chan, 2017; Gil de Zúñiga & Diehl, 2019; Gil de Zúñiga, Weeks, et al., 2017; Hao et al., 2014; Lee, 2020; Park & Kaye, 2019), or measures for Facebook (Cacciatore et al., 2018; David et al., 2019; Edgerly et al., 2018; Erkel & Van Aelst, 2020; Woo Yoo & Gil de Zúñiga, 2014) and Twitter (Edgerly et al., 2018; Erkel & Van Aelst, 2020; Woo Yoo & Gil de Zúñiga, 2014) news use. Some studies have focused on more specific issues, such as using social media to get campaign information (Ohme, 2020) or exposure to political information (Naderer et al., 2020; Wolfsfeld et al., 2016).

Regardless of the diversity of the approaches, results remain mixed as to whether researchers applied general social media use for news/information measures or specific ones (e.g., Facebook or Twitter news), thus making it difficult to calibrate the (potential) influence of social media news on political knowledge. In contrast to effects on participation, no distinct influences, such as incidental news exposure (Feezell & Ortiz, 2019), emerged to produce consistent effects. Several experiments and surveys concerning the intervening influence of mood on the relationship of incidental exposure to news, as well as social media news use and knowledge presented by Heiss and Matthes (2021), lead to no significant results. Park and Kaye (2019), however, found a positive influence of both social media news elaboration and news curation on political knowledge, highlighting that social media news use in interaction with political interest and political efficacy also produced a positive impact.

3.2.4 Interpersonal Communication

Despite evidence supporting a positive connection between people's interpersonal discussion attributes and political knowledge gain (Hopp et al., 2020; Li et al., 2016), studies that apply more general measurement instruments yielded null effects, or statistical nonsignificant results (Cacciatore et al., 2018; Naderer et al., 2020) – regardless whether these attributes for discussion are network size, heterogeneity, or political discussion. Specific platform measurements, such as Facebook discussion (Molaei, 2018) or Facebook network heterogeneity (Hopp et al., 2020), however, showed a promising positive influence on political knowledge, while the number of (Facebook) friends (network size) appeared to have no influence (Cacciatore et al., 2018; Naderer et al., 2020).

Since there are currently fewer studies in this area, these connections need to be further investigated before more precise conclusions can be drawn. The literature should especially help parse out the potential positive connection when platform-specific measurements are used. More research is needed to uncover how to best tap into the potential social networking sites offer citizens when it comes to learning more about politics.

3.2.5 Expressive Political Content

Similar to the effects of expressing political content over political participation, expression is also seen as the independent variable in some studies concerning knowledge, in addition to being applied as the dependent variable in others (Barnidge et al., 2018; Kim et al., 2020). Expressive behaviors have, furthermore, been linked with cognitive elaboration (Eveland, 2004; Yoo et al., 2017) which is a variable regularly associated with heightened political knowledge (Eveland, 2002; Eveland & Thomson, 2006; Jung et al., 2011). Several studies highlight a positive influence of expressive actions on political knowledge (Chen & Chan, 2017; Houston et al., 2013; Jennings et al., 2017; Valenzuela et al., 2019), while Cacciatore et al. (2018) reported a negative influence found with two different datasets.

However, the measurements for expression vary substantially across studies including general social media political expression (Chen & Chan, 2017) issue tweeting (Jennings et al., 2017), sharing on WhatsApp (Valenzuela et al., 2019), general tweeting (Houston et al., 2013), or (Facebook) news sharing (Cacciatore et al., 2018), making it difficult to compare the outcomes. Future research, thus, needs to pay attention to uniform, robust measurements to produce meaningful results. Political knowledge is similarly measured (Barnidge et al., 2018; Cacciatore et al., 2018; Chen & Chan, 2017; Kim et al., 2020; Valenzuela et al., 2019), except for a few more intricate captures, such as debate knowledge (Houston et al., 2013) or knowledge acquisition (Jennings et al., 2017).

3.2.6 Structural Effects

When it comes to political knowledge, there is a growing corpus of studies applying structural variables (Woo Yoo & Gil de Zúñiga, 2014), but the accumulated wisdom is nevertheless far less clear than for political participation. The few studies dealing with structural variables highlight ideology, as well as education as influential factors. While education in interaction with Facebook use positively predicts both civic and issue knowledge, no significant effects were found for education and Twitter (Woo Yoo & Gil de Zúñiga, 2014). So far, what is growingly highlighted by extant research is the moderating influence of ideology. Politically conservative people are more prone to encounter disinformation (Hjorth & Adler-Nissen, 2019). Non-Trump voters, for instance, have a significant chance of increasing campaign knowledge via Twitter, while Facebook is non-significant, and YouTube is even negatively correlated. For Trump voters, no significant effects were found for any of the three (Kanihan & Rim, 2018).

3.2.7 Miscellanea

Many studies in this literature review applied general or overall social media measures (e.g., number of hours spent on social media) and could, thus, not be associated with any of the aforementioned categories. Most studies, however, have non-significant results for the influence on political knowledge (Beckers et al., 2020; Gil de Zúñiga, 2012; Gil de Zúñiga, Weeks, et al., 2017; Kamau, 2017; Naderer et al., 2020; Park, 2019; Park & Kaye, 2019; Pasek et al., 2009). Despite some positive tendencies appearing in studies (Alam et al., 2019; Bode, 2016; Boukes, 2019; Gottfried et al., 2017), many researchers found negative influence of general social media use on political knowledge (Andı et al., 2020; Boukes, 2019; Cacciatore et al., 2018; Lee, 2019; Lee & Xenos, 2019). Once more, results presented by researchers thus far offer no conclusive direction or strength concerning the effect of social media use on political knowledge.

4 More Participation, Less Knowledge

4.1 Introduction

Prior sections have described the results from systematic literature reviews delving into the main effects that social media news use has on two variables that are key for liberal democracies: political knowledge and political participation. Those sections highlight two interrelated findings. Overall, using social media to consume information is (1) associated with higher levels of political participation, but (2) *not* associated with higher levels of political knowledge. Aggregated research efforts thus suggest that using social media makes individuals more participative, but not more knowledgeable; indeed, social media may even make individuals learn *less* compared to citizens who consume traditional media. Although many of these studies do not employ panel data that allows for causal analyses, the associations identified are highly suggesting a *Social Media Democracy Mirage*.

In the current section, we use survey data originally collected in the USA over the past decade at four points in time – 2009, 2013, 2015, and 2019 – to further sustain our claim related to the unfulfilled expectations of social media to promote and sustain democracy. We focus on the association between batteries of items consistently designed to measure social media news use, political participation, and political knowledge in a systematic way facilitating comparable and sound results from over a decade of increasing social media use.

We consider the relationship between our variables in multiple ways, using simple correlations, K-mean algorithmic clustering, and ordinary least squares (OLS) regressions. In each case, as we shall see, our findings support the storyline outlined above. Individuals who use social media for news more often are also more likely to engage in political activities. However, social media news use is not associated with higher levels of political knowledge; in fact, we find evidence of a *negative* association between social media use and political knowledge.

4.2 Data

Data for the analyses come from four online surveys conducted in the USA in 2009, 2013, 2015, and 2019. In all cases, a quota sampling strategy was followed so the final sample, extracted from an opt-in panel, reflected census characteristics such as gender and age. All surveys included questions to measure social media news use, political participation, and political knowledge. Although the measurement of these variables slightly varies over time (also reflecting refinements and developments in the field), the final constructs are easily comparable attending to the underlining concepts, which is a key advantage of the analysis.

4.2.1 The 2009 Dataset

The collection period for this dataset was from December 15, 2008, to January 5, 2009. The collection was overseen by a research unit hosted by the School of Journalism at the University of Texas at Austin in the USA, the Community Journalism & Mass Communication Research (CJCR), and the final survey was administered with Qualtrics. In order to obtain the desired sample size, a 10,000-random draw was matched for demographic characteristics. After eliminating invalid email addresses, 1,159 respondents remained as fully valid cases. The response rate calculated according to the American Association of Public Opinion Research's (AAPOR) RR3 amounts to 22.8 percent (American Association of Public Opinion Research, 2008, pp. 34–35). In comparison with the US census, the final sample was slightly better educated and had a lower proportion of males. More information on the comparison with the census can be found in Gil de Zúñiga and Valenzuela (2011).

Measurements

Social Media News Use

We used the average of the responses to these four statements about social media (1) It helps me stay informed about current events and public affairs, (2) It allows me to stay informed about my local community, (3) I use it to get news about current events from mainstream media such as CNN or ABC, (4) I use it to get news about current events through my friends and family (Cronbach's $\alpha = 0.87$, $M = 3.7$, $SD = 2.45$).

Political Participation

We used eight items: During the past year, have you (1) attended a public hearing, town hall meeting, or city council meeting? (2) called or sent a letter to an elected public official? (3) attended a political rally? (4) participated in any demonstrations, protests, or marches? (5) voted in the 2008 presidential election? (6) written a letter or email to a news organization? (7) participated in groups that took any local action for social or political reform? (8) been involved in public interest groups, political action groups, political clubs, or party committees? (Cronbach's $\alpha = 0.78$, M = 0.29, SD = 0.25).

Political Knowledge

We considered the correct responses to four questions about politics and averaged the scale: (1) Who is the British Prime Minister? (2) Who is the Speaker of the US House of Representatives? (3) Who is the Vice President-elect of the USA? (4) Sarah Palin is the governor of which state? (Guttman's $\lambda = 0.48$, M = 0.76, SD = 0.25).

4.2.2 The 2013 Dataset

This data was collected between December 15, 2013, and January 5, 2014. The collection process was overseen by the Digital Media Research Program (DMRP) at the University of Texas at Austin and administered with Qualtrics. After an initial sample comprising 5,000 people, 2,060 responded, while 247 cases were incomplete or had missing data. The response rate according to the AAPOR calculator was 34.6 percent. In contrast to the US Census, this sample is slightly younger, more educated, and included a lesser number of Hispanics. For more information on the census comparison breakdown, please see Saldaña, Mcgregor, and Zúñiga (2015).

Measurements

Social Media News Use

We used five questions: (1) How often do you use Facebook for getting news? (2) How often do you use Twitter for getting news? (3) How often do you use social media to stay informed about current events and public affairs (4) How often do you use social media to stay informed about the local community (5) How often do you use social media to get news about current events from mainstream media (e.g., CNN or ABC) (Cronbach's $\alpha = 0.87$, M = 2.88, SD = 2.14).

Political Participation

We used eight items to measure political participation in the prior three months: How often have you (1) attended/watched a public hearing, neighborhood, or school meeting? (2) contacted an elected public official? (3) attended a political rally? (4) participated in any demonstrations, protests, or marches? (5) participated in groups that took any local action for social or political reform? (6) been involved in public interest groups, political action groups, political clubs, political campaigns, or political party committees? (7) written a letter to the editor of a newspaper? (8) voted in federal or presidential elections? (Cronbach's $\alpha = 0.87$, M = 0.35, SD = 0.31).

Political Knowledge

We used five questions for political knowledge: (1) On which of the following does the US federal government currently spend the least? (2) Do you happen to know whether the immigration bill before Congress was introduced? (3) Do you happen to know what the ruling of the Supreme Court about Obamacare was? (4) Which organization's documents were released by Edward Snowden? (5) Recently, the United Nations (UN) and the USA were in negotiations with the Syrian government over the removal of what? (Guttman's $\lambda = 0.56$, M = 0.48, SD = 0.30).

4.2.3 The 2015 Dataset

This dataset was collected in the course of the Word Digital Influence Project, which was a collaboration between a research group based at Massey University in New Zealand and the Media Innovation Lab (MiLab) at the University of Vienna, Austria. The survey was administered by the MiLab at the University of Vienna and Qualtrics from September 14 to 24, 2015. The study included data from twenty-two countries. However, this Element only used data from the USA for its analyses (N = 1,161). The overall cooperation rate for this dataset was rather high, averaging 77 percent (American Association of Public Opinion Research, 2016). For more information on the data distribution and comparison to the census, please see Gil de Zúñiga and Liu (2017).

Measurements

Social Media News Use

We used four questions to see how (1) people get news from social media, as well as use social media to (2) stay informed about current events and public affairs, (3) stay informed about my local community, and (4) get news about current events from mainstream media (e.g., professional news services) (Cronbach's $\alpha = 0.90$, M = 3.41, SD = 1.69).

Political Participation

We used seven items in 2015. Listed below are some activities that you may or may not have engaged offline: (1) attended a meeting to discuss neighborhood problems, (2) contacted an elected public official, (3) attended a political rally, participated in any demonstrations, protests, or marches, (4) participated in groups that took any local action for social or political reform, (5) donated money to a campaign or political cause (6) signed up online to volunteer to help with a political cause, as well as (7) Usually, as far as you can recall, how often do you vote in national or presidential elections? (Cronbach's $\alpha = 0.85$, M = 0.36, SD = 0.31).

Political Knowledge

We included three questions in the 2015 survey questionnaire: (1) Who is the current Secretary-General of the United Nations? (2) What international organization is in charge of monitoring the use of nuclear energy throughout the world? (3) You might have heard some people talking about global warming. In your mind global warming is . . . (Guttman's $\lambda = 0.59$, M = 0.49, SD = 0.30).

4.2.4 The 2019 Dataset

This data was collected in June after research firm Ipsos Austria was contracted to provide respondents for the survey which was administered using Qualtrics. Matching the sample to key demographic data from the USA, 3,000 individuals were invited, resulting in a total of 1,338 valid cases. The cooperation rate calculated according to AAPOR amounts to 45.5 percent (American Association of Public Opinion Research, 2011). For more information on how the sample compares to the census, please see Gil de Zúñiga et al. (2021).

Measurements

Social Media News Use

We used five questions to assess this construct. In the past month, how often did you use the following social media sites for getting news? (1) Facebook (2) Twitter. Thinking of the social media you use the most, how often do you use it for the following activities? (3) to stay informed about current events and public affairs (4) to stay informed about my local community (5) to get news about current events from mainstream media (such as CNN or ABC) (Cronbach's $\alpha = 0.85$, M = 4.7, SD = 2.49).

Political Participation

We combined eight items to measure political participation: (1) How often do you do vote in federal or presidential elections? How often you have been involved in the following activities in the past 12 months: (2) attended/watched a public hearing, neighborhood or (3) contacted an elected public official (4) attended a political rally (5) participated in any demonstrations, protests, or marches (6) participated in groups that took any local action for political reform (7) been involved in public interest groups, political action groups, political clubs, political campaigns, or political party committees (8) wrote a letter to the editor of a newspaper? (Cronbach's $\alpha = 0.91$, $M = 0.46$, $SD = 0.37$).

Political Knowledge

We used eight items to capture knowledge: (1) What job or political office does Mike Pence currently hold? (2) For how many years is a US senator elected – that is, how many years are there in one full term of office for a US Senator? (3) What job or political office does Brett Kavanaugh currently hold? (4) On which of the following does the US federal government currently spend the least? (5) Do you happen to know whether the "For the People Act" bill before Congress was introduced? (6) Which of the following do you think most accurately describes the system of government used in the USA? (7) The WikiLeaks founder Julian Assange was arrested in London to face a charge in the USA of conspiring to hack into a Pentagon computer network in 2010. He had been living in the embassy of which country, which had sheltered him since 2012? (8) Which presidential candidate accused a liberal think tank of undermining Democrats' chances of taking back the White House in 2020 by "using its resources to smear" contenders? (Guttman's $\lambda = 0.73$, $M = 0.35$, $SD = 0.25$).

4.3 Associations Between Social Media News Use, Political Participation, and Political Knowledge

We begin by examining the bivariate correlations between our variables of interest, in each of the years during which data were gathered. Table 1 includes the results (a visual representation of Table 1 can be found in Figure 2A). A consistent and positive correlation between social media

Table 1 Correlation table. Social Media News Use (SMNU), political participation, and political knowledge.

	SMNU 2009	**SMNU 2013**	**SMNU 2015**	**SMNU 2019**
Political Participation	.231**	.351**	.245**	.300**
Political Knowledge	–.065	–.097**	–0.09**	–.132**

Note: Pearson correlation coefficients; Significance codes **0.01 *0.05.

news use and political participation was found in all four waves (the highest correlation coefficient in 2013, the lowest one in 2009). Conversely, social media news use was either nonsignificantly correlated with political knowledge (in 2009), or was negatively associated with it (2013–2019; the association is the strongest in the 2019 dataset). These preliminary results do not only underline the incapacity of social media news use to increase political knowledge, but they also suggest that the relationship is negative, in line with a number of studies considered in Section 3 (Cacciatore et al., 2018; Chen & Chan, 2017; Erkel & Van Aelst, 2020; Gil de Zúñiga, Weeks, et al., 2017; Heiss & Matthes, 2021; Lee, 2020).

As an additional test for examining the bivariate relationships between social media use and both participation and knowledge, we employed a K-means algorithmic cluster analysis. This technique is widely used to enable clustering of unstructured data by leveraging Euclidean distances among all data points (Likas et al., 2003). In short, this technique offers a valuable and alternative 'robustness mechanism check' to reassess how the data might cluster, using our variables of interest as reference points (see, e.g., Gil de Zúñiga et al., 2023). Before conducting this analysis, we rescaled the original measure for knowledge to ensure all variables fell within the same range (from 0 to 1). Subsequently, using SPSS software, we executed two separate K-means clustering analyses: the first incorporating social media news use and political participation, and the second involving social media news use and political knowledge. Moreover, for each year within the sample, we performed an individual analysis to classify the relationship among our variables of interest. The primary aim of this analysis was to ascertain whether respondents from the four different samples clustered in a similar manner. Rather than observing linear relationships as found in the bivariate associations, the K-mean clustering offers comparisons of the distributions as clusters of social media news use, participation (positively), and political knowledge (negatively) across four different US samples over a decade.

In terms of the testing between social media news use and political participation, respondents clustered into two distinct groups. The first group exhibited higher overlapping levels in both social media news use and political participation, while the second group showed lower levels in both aspects. Similarly, concerning social media news use and political knowledge, individuals with higher levels of social media news use consistently grouped with subjects also displaying lower levels of political knowledge. The adequacy of the two-cluster solution proposed varied between fairly good and highly suitable across all models, with silhouette coefficients consistently exceeding 0.5, which suggests a robust ratio of cohesion/

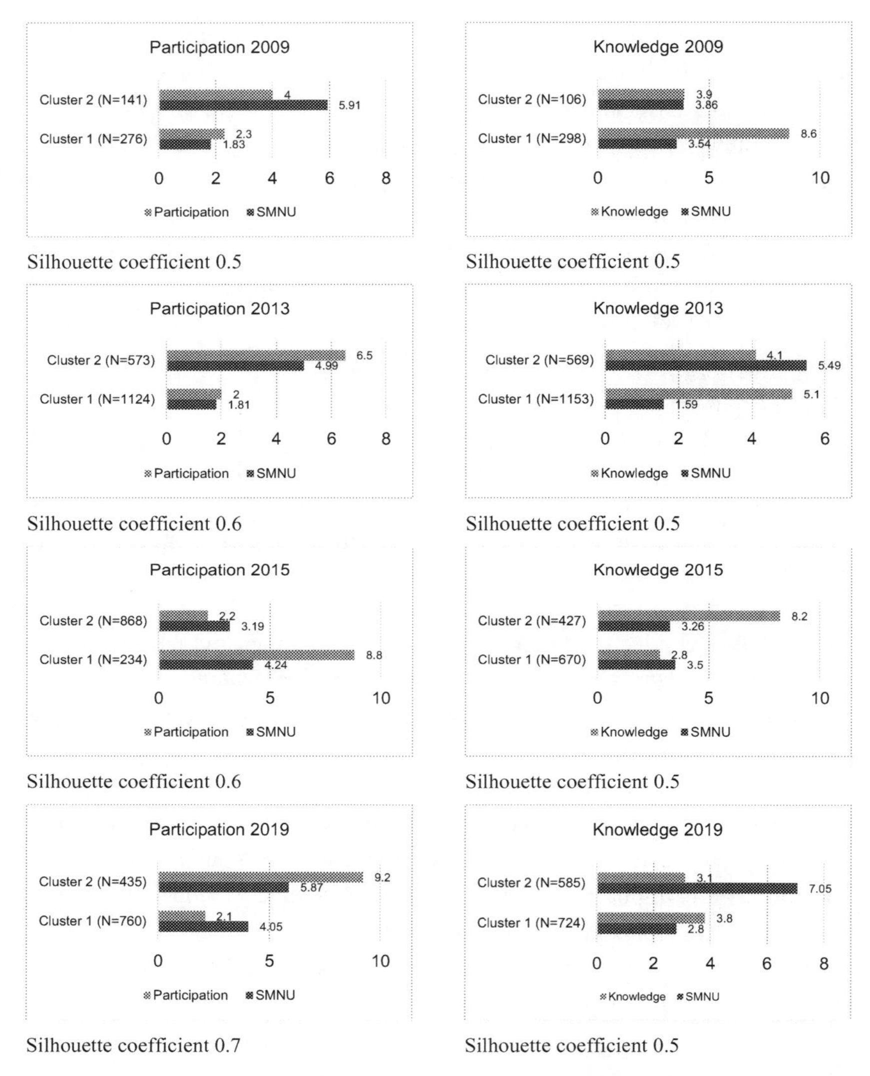

Figure 10 Descriptive data of the K-Mean Cluster Analysis.

separation among the clusters. The closer to 1, the better (Yuan & Yang, 2019). Descriptive statistics for the various clusters are provided in Figure 10. In the initial stage of K-means cluster analysis, the data is algorithmically divided into two clusters as the best fit. This clustering remains consistent across different years of data collection – 2009, 2013, 2015, and 2019 – where all data points consistently form two clusters. For

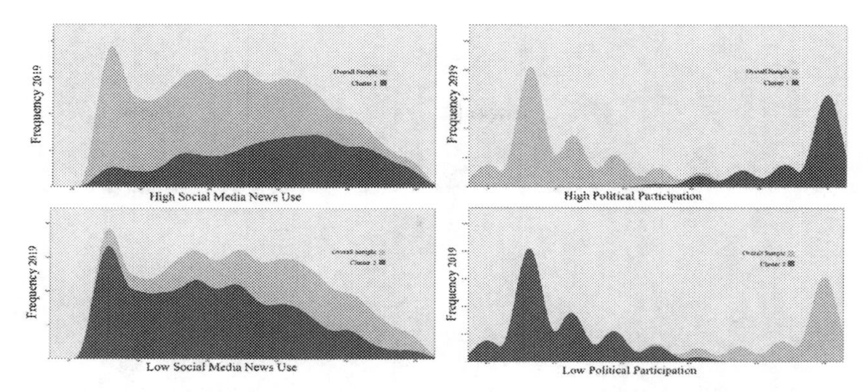

Figure 11 K-Means cluster algorithm data distributions for social media news use and political participation in 2019.

Note. The data visualization compares 2019 Overall Sample of Social Media News Use and Political Participation Distributions within the two clusters. Top figures correspond to Cluster 1: High Social Media Use and High Political Participation. Bottom figures represent Cluster 2: Low Social Media News Use and Low Political Participation.

example, in the analysis of social media news use and political participation, two distinct clusters emerge. Similarly, when examining social media news use and political knowledge, a two-cluster solution is also obtained. As depicted in Figure 10, one cluster comprises data points with lower levels of social media news use overlapping with those exhibiting lower levels of political participation. Conversely, a second cluster consists of data points suggesting higher levels of social media news use, which tend to coincide with higher levels of political participation. Regarding political knowledge, the two clusters indicate how frequent social media news use overlaps with less political knowledge, particularly evident in the 2009 and 2013 datasets. A visual and graphical representation of the most recent available data (2019) can be found in Figures 11 to 12 (figures for all other years are available in Figures 3A to 5A and 7A to 9A). This data visualization compares the distributions of social media news use and political participation within two clusters, based on the 2019 overall sample. The top figures highlight Cluster 1, distinguished by bold red colors indicating high levels of both social media use and political participation, while the softer tone of red in the background represents the distribution of the entire dataset. This allows for a clear comparison between cluster distributions and the overall sample. Conversely, the bottom figures display Cluster 2, characterized by bold red colors indicating low levels of both social media news use

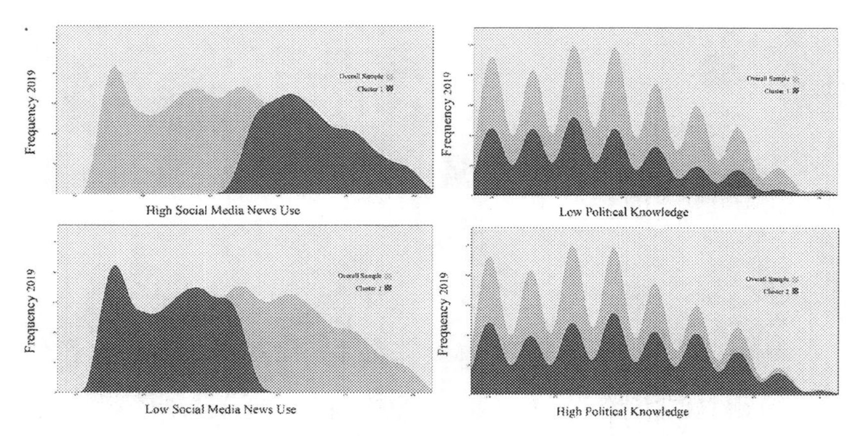

Figure 12 K-Means cluster algorithm data distributions for social media news use and political knowledge in 2019.

Note. The data visualization compares the 2019 overall sample of Social Media News Use and Political Knowledge Distributions within the two clusters. Top figures correspond to Cluster 1: High Social Media Use and High Political Knowledge. Bottom figures represent Cluster 2: Low Social Media News Use and Low Political Knowledge.

and political participation, contrasting with the entire distribution depicted in pale red in the background.

Overall, as we have seen in Table 1, an initial bivariate relationship test among SMNU, political participation, and political knowledge established a foundational linear association across all these variables of interest. Furthermore, the K-means algorithmic tests revealed the relationships between these variables more organically and intuitively, presenting a relatively less supervised machine learning model. The findings exposed consistent clusters across the years but indicated frequency differences within these clusters (refer to Figure 12 and 4A–9A). Lastly, to complement this methodological approach, we conducted a series of ordinary least squares (OLS) regressions using social media news use as an independent variable. Our dependent variables were political participation and political knowledge, and a different analysis was run for each year in which data is available (eight models in total). In order to show the basic association between variables, we ran simple OLS regression models that control for general news use as well as sociodemographic variables (i.e., gender, education, age, and income). These multivariate models confirm what we now know from bivariate analyses: There are associations between SMNU and participation and political knowledge beyond the effect of other individual uses of news media, and demographic characteristics.

Although political knowledge could have been measured as a 'count variable,' and therefore, another type of regression could have been pursued (i.e.,

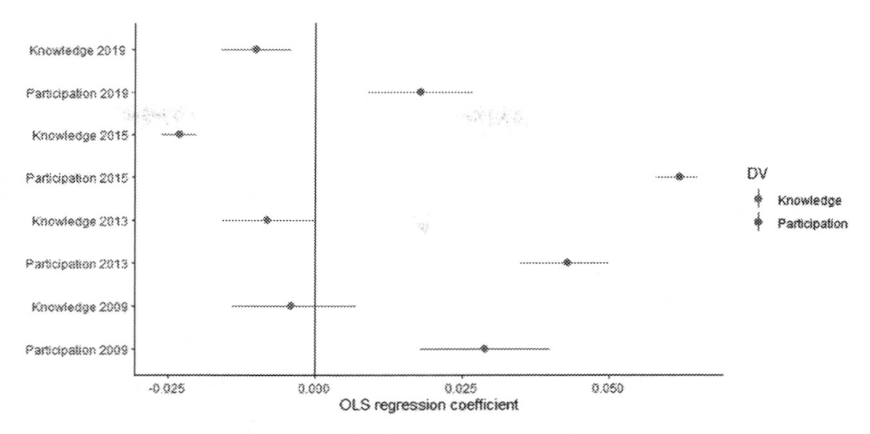

Figure 13 OLS regression coefficients.
Note. Points are B coefficients from the regression models and horizontal bars represent 95% confidence intervals.

negative binomial, Poisson regressions, etc.), we deemed our approach to be more theoretically nuanced as we do not imply the same human ability for each of the correct political knowledge items. That way, we use an overall index of political knowledge based on Guttman's Lambda since this statistic would account for differences in the variance that is due to true scores, and when test-takers may differ in their abilities, the λ-2 will be inexorably high, and the error will be low (Estabrook & Neale, 2013; Osburn, 2000).The results shown below (Figure 13) support this book's main claim: While higher levels of social media news use predict more political participation in all four waves considered in the analysis, the effects are negative for political knowledge in three out of four waves (there is no significant effect in 2009 even if the estimated average effect remains negative).

4.4 Conclusion

Our analysis of the US original data spanning over a decade largely supports that social media news use correlates positively with political participation. However, it is not associated with political knowledge or, whenever it does, the association is negative. The underlining reasons for these opposite trends have been considered in detail in the previous sections and can be summarized as follows. Social media news use creates and reinforces information networks that end up impacting the likelihood to take an active role regarding politics, in its many different forms. However, the information available, although important to trigger participation, seems to be either little reliable or unable to improve the objective political knowledge of people to the same extent that traditional news outlets do. The implications of these findings are discussed in the final section of this Element.

5 Final Conclusions

5.1 Democratic Impact

It becomes clear in the evolution of measurements and the addition of new items that the internet in general, and social media in particular, has changed how politics are conducted and experienced. Citizens can gather information, contact officials, or sign petitions without leaving their homes. Those in power also use the internet by implementing online campaigns or by directly communicating with their constituents and potential voters.

News and information consumption on social media has proven to have an overwhelmingly positive influence on participation. Social media also allows users to easily accumulate a large network that is often more heterogenous than their offline contacts tend to be. In several studies, network size and heterogeneity are linked with increased participation. Being able to express oneself politically on social media has emerged as another influential factor in participation.

While these findings seemingly attest to the grand positive impact social media has brought to politics, it also appears that several offline issues persist online. There is still a gender divide in participation, although many expected the internet to act as an equalizer. Even in online spaces, women tend to participate less or at least differently than men. Despite the internet and social media offering a cheap way of becoming engaged in politics, as opposed to offline participation, higher income is a predictor of political participation even in the online realm. Only a few studies support the hope that economically disadvantaged people would profit more from these new online affordances. Additionally, the connection between social media, education, and participation is mixed, showing no clear direction.

Overall, and even if inequalities remain, social media appears to have a big positive democratic impact by providing citizens with easily accessible information and news, providing a space for discussion and deliberation, and giving them room to express themselves politically. However, when it comes to political knowledge, the results look rather different. No matter which research area the focus lies on, no distinct direction of the impact on knowledge could be pinned down. Whether it is social media news consumption, political discussion, or political expression, the results are inconclusive with just as many studies providing positive results as there are negative and nonsignificant ones (Amsalem & Zoizner, 2023). So, despite the positive influence social media has on participation, this is not the case for political knowledge. At best, social media does not really impact knowledge. But at worst, it can even be damaging to the democratic process by decreasing people's political knowledge. However, where does this leave social media use in relation to the functioning of democracies? Or, to put it in different words, is the promotion of participation among less knowledgeable individuals positive for democracy?

One way to respond to this question is to pay attention to the positive effects of social media news use (i.e., more participation) and discard the rest. In that vein, social media news use will be no panacea for democracies because more knowledge is not guaranteed, but at least we will see some participation shortcomings addressed. This approach is in line with the unfulfilled expectations of social media in the context of democratic ideals. An alternative approach is to consider that the promotion of participation among less knowledgeable individuals is not only far from perfect, but an issue in its terms. In that sense, individuals who display low levels of political knowledge are much more likely to vote for candidates and parties that do not represent their preferences (Arnold, 2012; Bartels, 1996; Fowler & Margolis, 2014), do not punish corrupt politicians (Klašnja, 2017), override informed group decisions (Großer & Seebauer, 2016), and fail in the cost-benefit calculation process associated with collective action (Chwe, 1999; Paige, 1971). Likewise, individuals' low levels of political knowledge limit some potential advantages of deliberation (Jennings, 2019; Somin, 2006) and complicate identifying which policy preferences are more in agreement with their own judgments (Gilens, 2001).

What is worse, social media use for news fosters the illusion of knowledge as an individual will develop the perception that the "news will find me," without being active or surveillant about public affairs information (Gil de Zúñiga et al., 2017). Citizens will mistakenly believe they are knowledgeable about politics without doing anything about it, as the news will find them. Accepting that political knowledge is to democratic politics what money is to economics, the currency of citizenship (Delli Carpini & Keeter 1996: p. 8), low levels of political knowledge in a society posit important challenges for the functioning of democracies. Some of these challenges can be aggravated when lower levels of political knowledge are combined with high participation.

In this vein, rational ignorance theory predicts that some individuals may choose not to be informed about politics because of the costs associated with more knowledge (Somin, 2019). In contexts where too much information about public affairs is available, an increasing amount of people may choose to stay away from political news not because they do not care at all about it, but because of time and/or intellectual constraints, practicing news avoidance (Skovsgaard & Andersen, 2020), which may be distinct to sheer information overload (Goyanes et al., 2021). Although rational ignorance has been said to have some positive effects (e.g., it may liberate time for altruistic individuals to take part in social activities that are beneficial for people other than themselves), a general agreement exists on the negative consequences of political ignorance for participation in representative democracies (Somin, 2014; 2019). This further supports our claim of a democratic mirage derived from social media news use, unless alternative mechanisms exist that allow uninformed individuals to make decisions that are in line with their interests.

A well-established line of research in political psychology revolving around shortcuts and cognitive heuristics has shown that even uninformed individuals are sometimes able to make decisions that are in line with their preferences (Schaffner & Streb, 2002). For example, individuals can use party labels as an effective cue for voting even if they do not know the specific policy positioning of candidates in a given election or look at what a group of interest with which they are often in agreement is saying about a topic that is new to them. Even relatively well-informed individuals are likely to recur to heuristics from time to time due to the (increasingly) unmanageable amount of information that is available (Kuklinski & Quirk, 2000).

Effective heuristics could be a challenge to our main thesis, given that the negative effects of social media news use in political knowledge could be heavily cushioned. However, while acknowledging the importance of heuristics in different situations, we believe that important shortcomings associated with them reinforce our democracy mirage approach (e.g., policy stereotypes, the influence of easy arguments, or biased processing of information). Basically, even if a small amount of political information could be used as a compass to navigate complex political discussions when cues are operating – the imperfect processing of that information is likely to cause additional troubles.

Political knowledge is far from solving all these problems, but it makes it more likely for individuals to behave in ways that are in agreement with their preferences. This can be seen in voting, but it has consequences well beyond, provided that accurate information can be key for signing certain petitions while declining others, taking part in demonstrations that are in the best interest of the individual, knocking on the door of the public representative who can help solve certain issues or prevent the spread of inaccurate and/or fake news.

Our democracy mirage claim should not be read as supporting an elitist understanding of democracy where only highly informed people participate, but rather as a warning about the blind spots that democratic systems may develop as the use of social media for news spread. Key in this regard is the cost of opportunity associated with social media news use, reducing the time available to get informed in more traditional media outlets that increase political knowledge (Chaffee & Kanihan, 1997; Delli Carpini & Keeter, 1996). Overall, individuals may not become less knowledgeable the more they consume news on social media, but this seems a plausible scenario unless additional sources of information are considered. At the very least no improvements in political knowledge are expected on average if additional sources of information beyond social media are lacking.

5.2 Suggestions for Future Research

The analyses conducted so far have identified different aspects that need further development and closer attention from researchers. For the most part, both knowledge and participation research suffer from the same issues that demand ameliorations. Those are, more saliently, the applied measurements, that need to be reinvestigated, updated, and refined. Moreover, there are several areas that are understudied and need more attention, such as qualitative aspects, network, and structural influences, as well as cross-country-differences.

5.2.1 Social Media and How It Is Measured

The first and biggest challenge revolves around the operationalization of social media. This is due to a variety of concepts within social media (e.g., news use, discussion, expression, etc.), which come up in various research and have different measurements. Even within these areas, the applied measures differ substantially (e.g., discussion network size, network heterogeneity, discussion frequency, etc.). In short, the researchers introduce different constructs to measure the same concepts and when they measure very similar, or if not the same phenomena, they use different items.

What is, thus, often summarized into positive or negative effects of social media news use on political knowledge and participation, come from the number of hours or the way people use those platforms to organize protest. While the variety of measurements does make it difficult to compare results, it also suggests that social media is many-facetted, and applying general measures is an oversimplification, at least to better explain some of the social media effects. Those measures produced mixed and at times negative results when it comes to participation (Gil de Zúñiga, 2012; Gil de Zúñiga, Copeland, et al., 2014b; Kamau, 2017; Pasek et al., 2009; Theocharis & Lowe, 2016b) or knowledge (Beckers et al., 2020; Gil de Zúñiga, Barnidge, et al., 2017; Park,

2019; Park & Kaye, 2019), while specific measures such as political (Choi & Kwon, 2019; Chon & Park, 2020; Gainous et al., 2020; Valenzuela, 2013; Vissers & Stolle, 2014a) or protest use (Bond et al., 2012; Costanza-Chock, 2012; Dey, 2020; Hamanaka, 2020; Joia & Soares, 2018; Maher & Earl, 2019) can lead to positive outcomes. In the case of political knowledge, only very specific measurements (e.g., political expression via WhatsApp or Facebook network heterogeneity) produced positive results.

Thus, in order to gauge an accurate and reliable picture of the influence of social media, the measurements need to be updated and specified. Since the first studies were conducted on SNS such as Facebook or Twitter, those platforms have changed and evolved, gaining new affordances that need to be accounted for and reflected (Valenzuela et al., 2018). These functions and distinct reasons for use might even vary across platforms (Facebook, Twitter, YouTube, etc.), thus researchers should apply separate measures for those as well. As can be seen from the literature review on knowledge, overall social media measures appeared to be noninfluential, whereas studies that disentangled the influence of social media platforms showcased more nuanced and positive findings.

This is a clear indicator that various mechanisms are at work depending on the platform and that citizens use those platforms differently as well. Hence, more attention needs to be paid to these details to get an accurate picture of any possible positive or negative influence. Thus, researchers need to develop and propagate more specific measurements by capturing the affordances of each social media platform and being consistent when applying them.

5.2.2 Political Participation?

Similar to social media, the measurements for political participation also vary across studies. This ranges from separate measures for online (Bode & Dalrymple, 2016; Chan et al., 2017; Chunly, 2019; Hoffman, 2012; Steinberg, 2015; Yamamoto et al., 2019) and offline participation (Garcia-Castañon et al., 2011; Gil de Zúñiga, Molyneux, et al., 2014; Kwak et al., 2018; Lane et al., 2017), or low and high effort participation (Nanz et al., 2020) to distinct captures for civic engagement (Zhang & Skoric, 2018), protest (Diehl et al., 2019; Karakaya & Glazier, 2019; Zumarraga-Espinosa, 2020), voting (Diehl et al., 2019; Hassim et al., 2020; Towner, 2013), campaign and party activities (Amaral et al., 2016; Ċogburn & Espinoza-Vasquez, 2011; Gerl et al., 2018; Housholder & LaMarre, 2013; Jensen, 2017; Jiang, 2017; Larsson, 2020; Penney, 2017; Ridge-Newman, 2020), activism (Gil de

Zúñiga et al., 2019; Zhang & Skoric, 2018), political expression (Chapman & Coffé, 2016) and consumerism (Gil de Zúñiga, 2012; Kim & Chen, 2015; Zhang & Skoric, 2018).

While some researchers focus on one or several of these measures, others use an overall participation measurement that includes and combines some of these aspects (Graham et al., 2020; Lee & Xenos, 2020; Shaw et al., 2020). With such a variety of outcome variables, it is difficult to compare the effects. What is, however, evident, is that there is merit in such specific measures allowing us to differentiate possible distinct influence and effects. Previous research has shown that online and offline participation are different concepts, so if anything, at least this distinction should be made (Gibson & Cantijoch, 2013; Gil de Zúñiga et al., 2010; Kim et al., 2017; Oser et al., 2013).

Additionally, the measurements should be updated and specified to reflect new forms of and developments in participation. For example, asking whether somebody contacted a government official has been included in the participation measures since before online participation became relevant. However, nowadays there are both online and offline ways of approaching certain participatory actions such as contacting (e.g., via social media or writing an email in addition to writing letters or calling a number, wearing a campaign button or sticker and changing a profile picture, discussing politics online and offline). Thus, research needs some measurements that reflect these intricate nuances and developments instead of combining them all into one variable.

5.2.3 Structural Influence

When looking at the sample for the literature reviews on social media, political participation, and political knowledge, it becomes evident that structural influences are somewhat neglected. The studies that feature those elements highlight the possible impact of variables, such as gender (Morris & Morris, 2013; Vicente & Novo, 2014; Xenos et al., 2014), income (Bode & Dalrymple, 2016; Chunly, 2019; Garcia-Castañon et al., 2011), education (Ahmed & Cho, 2019; Bode, 2017), ideology (Hjorth & Adler-Nissen, 2019; Kanihan & Rim, 2018), or age (Bode, 2017; Chunly, 2019; Strandberg, 2014).

Results, however, are still largely inconclusive. Especially when it comes to different countries the effect of structural influences could vary substantially. For example, while SNSs were heralded as great equalizers when it comes to participating and manifesting big impacts during the Arab Spring, the results from various studies show that there are still stark differences based on gender or income that are not eradicated by social media. Several studies presented in our literature review show that gender differences might be more pronounced online. Thus, more extensive research is warranted to disentangle the intervening influence of structural factors. Additional results are needed to clarify which variables are important, in which direction the effect goes, and whether those effects hold across borders.

5.2.4 Network Effects

Studies considering people's social network attributes and its effects are overall scarce, and include different variables in the analyses (e.g., network heterogeneity, network size, political discussion with weak or strong ties, etc.). Considering that there are only a few more studies conducted in this area than on structural influences and the number of different variables, there is limited research on each of those factors to draw any robust inferences. Thus, more research is needed, also when it comes to different social media outlets (e.g., TikTok, YouTube, Facebook, Instagram, etc.), specifically for political knowledge measurements focusing on Facebook instead of overall social media highlight positive influence. Circling back to the first point in this section, this shows that more intricate measurements need to be applied to gauge the true influence of social media. We also encourage scholars to conduct more research on the effect of other social media like Twitter since not all effects occur the same way on each SNS.

5.2.5 US Centricity

The majority of studies in both literature reviews are from the USA. It is, however, important to highlight that many researchers concluded that such phenomena are not one-size-fits-all since different political situations and regimes across cultures could produce different results. Censorship, for instance, is more extreme in other countries than in the USA, thus substantially influencing what people can even access or express via social media. Considering that the USA has found itself in a rather unconventional situation in recent years due to President Donald Trump, the results might not be generalizable globally.

Especially when looking at political knowledge, the USA shows mostly negative or nonsignificant influence of social media (Barnidge et al., 2018; Cacciatore et al., 2018; Edgerly et al., 2018; Feezell et al., 2009; Feezell & Ortiz, 2019; Kanihan & Rim, 2018; Lee, 2020; Lee & Xenos, 2019; Pasek et al., 2009). However, other countries such as Iran (Alam et al., 2019), Indonesia (Astuti & Hangsing, 2018), Austria (Heiss & Matthes, 2021), China (Li et al., 2016), Zimbabwe (Mwonzora, 2020), Denmark (Ohme, 2020), South Korea (Park & Kaye, 2019), and Chile

(Valenzuela et al., 2019) show more positive results. This highlights how different outcomes can be, thus warranting more research focused outside of the USA.

5.2.6 Study Designs

Based on our close investigation of prior research, we recommend an update of study designs. First, the vast majority of studies feature quantitative designs. However, as prior research has shown how very distinct uses of social media can be impactful, more qualitative research (e.g., in-depth interviews, focus groups) is needed to further investigate those nuances. This could be vital to discover how, for example, Facebook and Twitter are used in contrast to each other (e.g., one platform might be preferred when discussing but the other for news). Additionally, that could also help distinguish different uses within one specific SNS (e.g., political or protest use of Facebook, etc.) and uncover potential new important applications of those SNSs. A better understanding of details would also allow for more precise and impactful measurements to be developed for quantitative designs.

Second, the most popular method among researchers is a survey, which means that data are from self-reported measurements. Other ways of assessing subjects' online behaviors such as (real-time) experiments need to be promoted. Finally, if quantitative survey research is conducted, we should strive for more panel data. The present research is mostly based on cross-sectional datasets which do not allow for lagged or autoregressive testing. We recommend the use of lagged or autoregressive analyses to get a more accurate idea of the strength of effects in time, and to investigate the dynamic influence that might occur.

5.3 All in All . . .

Overall, the comprehensive analysis presented in this book sheds light on the transformative impact of the internet and social media on the political realm, particularly regarding individuals' political behavior and acquisition of public affair news and knowledge. While social media provides convenient access to information and encourages political expression, it also preserves offline inequalities, especially regarding gender and socio-economic status. Despite its positive influence on political participation, social media (news use) effects on political knowledge remain ambiguous, at best. The proliferation of news on social media platforms may foster a false sense of political awareness, aggravating democratic challenges (see, e.g., the "News Finds Me" Perception Theory, Gil de Zúñiga & Cheng, 2021). While cognitive shortcuts like party affiliations offer some guidance, they may also reinforce biases and undermine an informed public opinion decision-making. Overall, we contend that enhancing political knowledge is key for cultivating an informed citizenry and mitigating the adverse effects of social media-driven politics. This Element underscores the need to address the limitations of social media, especially as a primary news source, and advocates for a balanced approach that integrates diverse information channels to uphold democratic values and foster strong civic literacy.

Appendix

Social Media and Political Participation

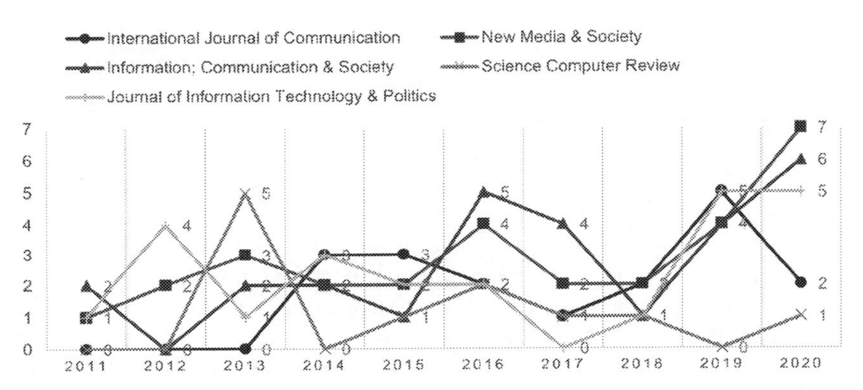

Figure 1A Number of publications in the top five journals with most published articles by year.

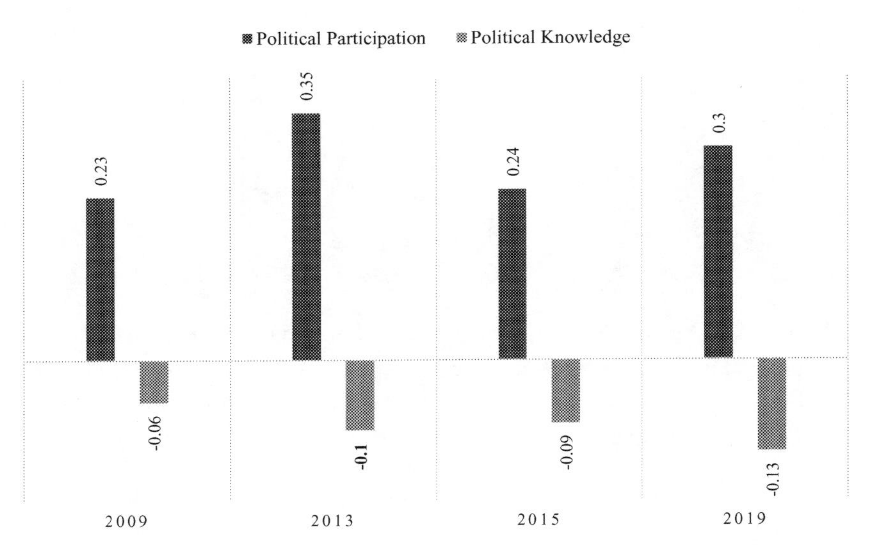

Figure 2A Pearson's correlation coefficients. Visualization from Table 1, Section 4. Social media news use, political participation, and political knowledge.

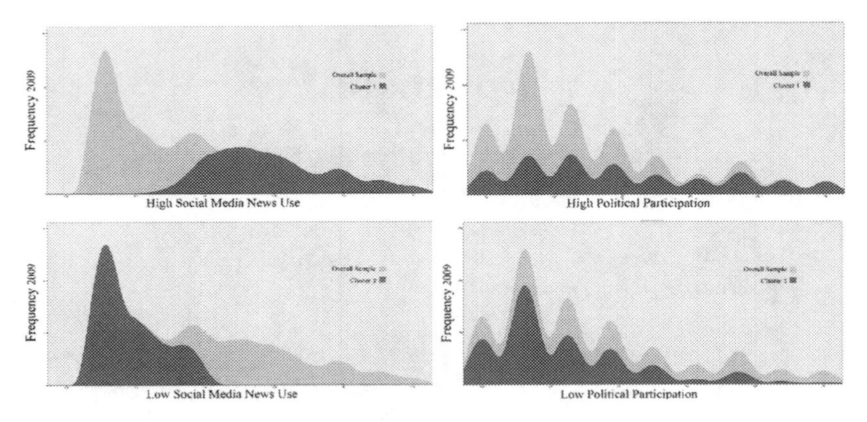

Figure 3A K-Means cluster algorithm data distributions for social media news use and political participation news and political participation in 2009.

Note. The data visualization compares 2009 Overall Sample of Social Media News Use and Political Participation Distributions within the two clusters. Top figures correspond to Cluster 1: High Social Media Use and High Political Participation. Bottom figures represent Cluster 2: Low Social Media News Use and Low Political Participation.

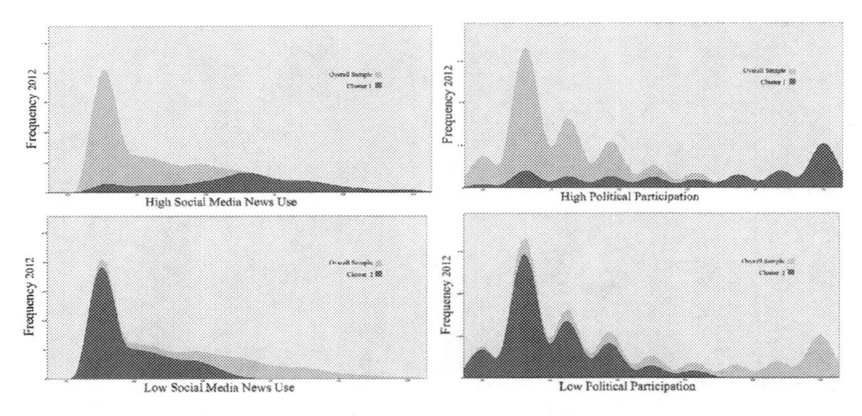

Figure 4A K-Means cluster algorithm data distributions for social media news use and political participation news and political participation in 2013.

Note. The data visualization compares 2013 Overall Sample of Social Media News Use and Political Participation Distributions within the two clusters. Top figures correspond to Cluster 1: High Social Media Use and High Political Participation. Bottom figures represent Cluster 2: Low Social Media News Use and Low Political Participation.

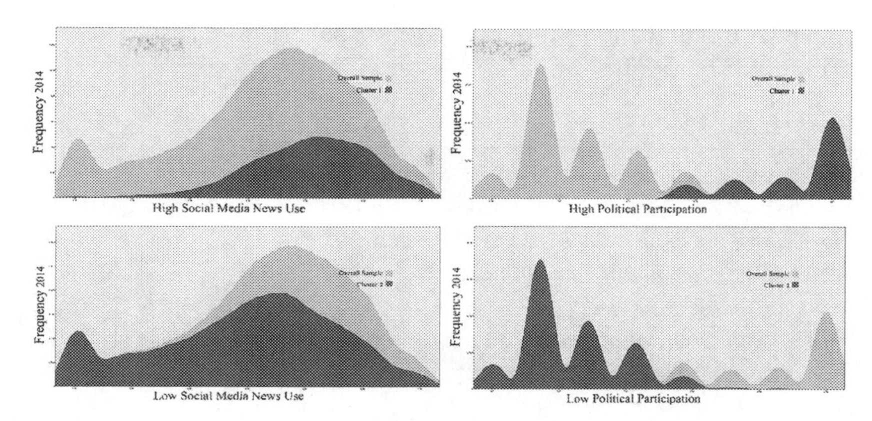

Figure 5A K-Means cluster algorithm data distributions for social media news use and political participation news and political participation in 2015.

Note. The data visualization compares 2015 Overall Sample of Social Media News Use and Political Participation Distributions within the two clusters. Top figures correspond to Cluster 1: High Social Media Use and High Political Participation. Bottom figures represent Cluster 2: Low Social Media News Use and Low Political Participation.

Table 1A List of journals for social media and political participation papers.

Journals	Number of articles
New Media & Society	31
Information Communication & Society	27
Journal of Information Technology & Politics	25
International Journal of Communication	18
Science Computer Review	12
International Journal of Press/Politics; *Journal of Broadcasting & Electronic Media*	11
Communication Research; *Media, Culture & Society*; *Social Media and Society*	7
Government Information Quarterly; *Information Communication & Society*; *Journal of Communication*; *Policy and Internet*; *Political Communication*	6
Journal of Youth Studies; *Journal of Political Marketing*; *Chinese Journal of Communication*; *Public Relations Review*; *Telematics and Informatics*	5
Asian Journal of Communication; Australian Journal of Political Science; *Communication & Society*; *Convergence; International Journal of Electronic Governance*; *Journalism and Mass Communication Quarterly*; *Malaysian Journal of Communication*	4
American Behavioral Scientist; *Communication Research Reports*; *Communication Studies*; *Digital Journalism*; *Korea Observer*; *Political Behavior*; *SAGE Open*; *The British Journal of Politics and International Relations*	3
African Journalism Studies; *Atlantic Journal of Communication*; *Communication Review*; *Computers in Human Behavior*; *Democratization*; *E-Journal of E-Democracy and Open Government*; *Electoral Studies*; *Feminist Media Studies*; *Geopolitics, History, and International Relations*; *Global Media and Communication*; *Information Polity*; International *Journal of Scientific and Technology Research*; *Journal of African Media Studies*; *Journal of Computer-Mediated Communication*; *Journal of Language and Politics*; *Journal of Media Psychology*; *KOME*; *Local Government Studies*; *Mass Communication and Society*; *Media International Australia*;	2

Table 1A (cont.)

Journals	Number of articles
Observatorio; *Political Research Quarterly*; *Politics*; *Quality and Quantity*; *Scandinavian Political Studies*; *Social Movement Studies*; *Social Science Journal*; *South East Asia Research*; *VOLUNTAS*	
Acta Política; *Adcomunica – Revista Científica de Estrategias Tendencias e Innovación en Comunicación*; *Africa Spectrum*; *Akdeniz Iletisim*; *Annals of the American Academy of Political and Social Science*; *Asian Journal of Political Science*; *Australian Journal of Psychology*; *Behaviour & Information Technology*; *British Journal of Social Psychology*; *Canadian Review of Sociology*; *Catalan Journal of Communication and Cultural Studies*; *Central Asia and the Caucasus*; *Children & Youth Services Review*; *Chinese Sociological Review*; *Citizenship Studies*; *Cogent Social Sciences*; *Communications: The European Journal of Communication Research*; *Comunicar*; *Critical Discourse Studies*; *Critical Sociology*; *Cuadernos Info*; *Demokratizatsiya*; *Doxa Comunicacion*; *East Asia: An International Quarterly*; *East European Politics & Societies*; *Electronic Government*; *Ethnos: Journal of Anthropology*; *Europe's Journal of Psychology*; *French Politics*; *Human Communication Research*; *Intellectual Discourse*; *International Journal of Criminology and Sociology*; *International Journal of Politics, Culture and Society*; *International Journal of Public Opinion Research*; *International Journal of Strategic Communication*; *International Journal of Web Based Communities*; *International Political Science Review*; *International Review of Administrative Sciences*; *Intersections East European Journal of Society and Politics*; *Javnost: The Public*; *Journal of Applied Journalism & Media Studies*; *Journal of Asian Public Policy*; *Journal of Baltic Studies*; *Journal of Behavioral Health Services & Research*; *Journal of Communication Inquiry*; *Journal of Consumer Culture*; *Journal of Contemporary African Studies*; *Journal of Contemporary China*; *Journal of Contemporary Ethnography*; *Journal of Content, Community and Communication*; *Journal of Ethnic and Migration Studies*;	1

Table 1A (cont.)

Journals	**Number of articles**
Journal of Muslims in Europe; *Journal of Political Power*; *Journal of Political Science Education*; *Journal of Public Affairs*; *Journal of Urban Affairs*; *Journalism Practice*; *Jurnal the Messenger*; *Kajian Malaysia: Journal of Malaysian Studies*; *Learning, Media and Technology*; *Media and Communication*; *Middle East Journal of Culture and Communication*; *Mind, Culture & Activity*; *Mobile Media & Communication*; *Nature*; *Nordicom Review*; *Palgrave Communications*; *Party Politics*; *Perspectives on Politics*; *Policy Studies*; *Political Psychology*; *Political Science Research and Methods*; *Political Studies*; *Problems of Post-Communism*; *Public Opinion Quarterly*; *Public Policy and Administration*; *Qualitative Inquiry*; *Daedalus*; *Qualitative Research*; *Rationality and Society*; *Revista de Cercetare si Interventie Sociala*; *Revista Espanola de Ciencia Política*; *Revista Latina de Comunicación Social*; *Romanian Journal of Political Science*; *Round Table*; *Social and Economic Studies*; *Social Identities*; *Social Science Quarterly*; *Social Semiotics*; *Information Technology for Development*; *Social Work* (United States); *Sociological Perspectives*; *Sociology*; *Stability*; *Studies in Communication Sciences*; *Technology in Society*; *Terrorism and Political Violence*; *The Journal of Legislative Studies*; *Third World Quarterly*; *Transforming Government: People, Process and Policy*; *Violence Against Women*; *Visual Communication*; *Young*	

Table 2A List of first author's country of origin for social media and political participation papers.

First author's country of origin	Number of papers
USA	154
UK	30
Hong Kong	21
Australia	19
Canada	17
Austria	15
Germany	14
Spain; Sweden	12
Italy	10
South Korea	9
India; Israel; Netherlands	8
Chile; China	7
Brazil; Denmark; Taiwan	6
Belgium; Finland; Malaysia; Nigeria	5
Indonesia; Ireland; Mexico; New Zealand; Norway; Portugal; Singapore; South Africa	4
Columbia; France; Hungary; Macau	3
Estonia; Pakistan; Poland; Russia; Switzerland; Turkey	2
Afghanistan; Croatia; Cyprus; Czech Republic; Ecuador; Egypt; Japan; Kazakhstan; Lithuania; Niger; North Korea; Northern Cyprus; Philippines; Zimbabwe	1

Table 3A List of countries of data collection for social media and political participation papers.

Country	Number of papers
USA	127
Multi-country	52
China	21
UK	19
South Korea	18
Sweden	11
Australia; Hong Kong; India	10
Canada; Germany; Spain	9
Austria; Not specified country	8
Chile; Denmark; Italy; Taiwan	7
Brazil; Israel; Nigeria	6
Belgium; Finland; Malaysia; Netherlands	5
Indonesia; Mexico; Singapore	4
Egypt; Ireland; Russia; Turkey; Zimbabwe	3
Bulgaria; Cambodia; Columbia; Croatia; Ethiopia; France; Greece; Hungary; Japan; Morocco; Pakistan; Philippines; South Africa; Ukraine	2
Afghanistan; Czech Republic; Ecuador; Estonia; Ghana; Iran; Kazakhstan; Lebanon; New Zealand; Nigeria; Northern Cyprus; Norway; Portugal; Switzerland; Uganda; Venezuela; Vietnam	1

Table 4A Most common measurement instruments for political participation online.

Number of items	Scale	Items	Used by
6	1–10	How often during the past twelve months did you engage or not in any of the following activities? • igned or shared an online petition • participated in online political polls • participated in an online question-and-answer session with a politician or public official • created an online petition • signed up online to volunteer to help with a political cause • used a mobile phone to donate money to a campaign or political cause via text message or app	(Saldaña et al., 2015)
4	1–4	How often during the past month did you engage or not in any of the following activities? • contacted a politician using emails or social media • signed an online petition • made an online campaign contribution • signed up to volunteer for an online campaign	(Park & Kaye, 2018a)

Table 4A (cont.)

Number of items	Scale	Items	Used by
5	0–10	How often during the past twelve months did you engage or not in any of the following activities? • written to a politician • made a campaign contribution • subscribed to a political listserv • signed up to volunteer for a political campaign • written to a news organization	(Gil de Zúñiga, Molyneux, et al., 2014)
6	0/1 per item, then recoded into low/high (0–5)	How often during the campaign did you engage or not in any of the following activities? • forwarded a political email to another person • talked to any people and tried to show them online why they should vote for or against one of the parties or candidates • followed or became a fan of a political candidate on a social network • posted a comment or weblink on a blog, social network, or website to express a political opinion • participated in online discussion or chat groups about politics • given an online donation to a candidate or political party.	(Towner, 2013)
7	1–5	How often during the past twelve months did you engage or not in any of the following activities? • registering one’s opinions by participating in online polls	(Zhang et al., 2013)

		• getting information about a candidate’s voting record • sending or receiving campaign-related emails • contributing money online to a candidate running for public office • looking for online information about candidates’ positions on the issues • finding out about endorsements or ratings of candidates by organizations or individuals online • checking the accuracy of claims made by or about the candidates online	
8	1–4	How often during the past twelve months did you engage or not in any of the following activities? • signed a petition via a link on Facebook; • helped collect signatures for a petition by sharing a link on your Facebook page • joined a political group on Facebook • showed your support for a cause, candidate, campaign and/or stand on an issue by liking a Facebook page • making a donation to a political group, candidate, and/or campaign via a link on Facebook • showed your support for a cause, candidate, campaign, political group and/or stand on an issue by sharing a link or post on Facebook • contacted an elected official via a link on Facebook • tried to persuade other people via Facebook to support a cause, candidate and/or stand on an issue	(Cao, 2020)

Table 5A Most common measurement instruments for political participation offline.

Number of items	Scale	Items	Used by
9	1–10	How often during the past twelve months did you engage or not in any of the following activities? • attended/watched a public hearing, neighborhood or school meeting • contacted an elected public official • attended a political rally • participated in any demonstrations, protests, or marches • donated money to a campaign or political cause • participated in groups that took any local action for social or political reform • been involved in public interest groups, political action groups, political clubs, political campaigns, or political party committees • voted in local/statewide elections • voted in federal/presidential elections	(Saldaña et al., 2015)
6	1–4	How often during the past month did you engage or not in any of the following activities? • posted a campaign sticker, banner, or button • called or sent a letter to an elected public official	(Park & Kaye, 2018a)

		• attended a political meeting, rally, or speech • worked for a political party or a candidate • contributed money to political campaigns or candidates • participated in groups that took any action for political reform	
7	0–10	How often during the past twelve months did you engage or not in any of the following activities? • attended a public hearing, town hall meeting, or city council meeting • called or sent a letter to an elected public official • spoken to a public official in person • attended a political rally • participated in any demonstrations, protests, or marches • participated in groups that took any local action for social or political reform • been involved in public interest groups, political action groups, political clubs, or party committees	(Gil de Zúñiga, Molyneux, et al., 2014)
5	0/1 per item, then recoded into low/high (0–5)	How often during the campaign did you engage or not in any of the following activities? • talked to any people and tried to show them why they should vote for or against one of the parties or candidates • gone to any political meetings, rallies, speeches, dinners, or things like that in support of a particular candidate	(Towner, 2013)

Table 5A (cont.)

Number of items	Scale	Items	Used by
		• worn a campaign button, put a campaign sticker on their car, or placed a sign in their window or in front of their house • worked for one of the parties or candidates • given an offline donation to a candidate or political party	
5	1–5	How often during the past twelve months did you engage or not in any of the following activities? • talking to people and trying to show them why they should vote for or against one of the parties or candidates • wearing a campaign button or putting a campaign sticker on one's car or placing a sign in one's window or in front of one's house • attending political meetings, rallies, or speeches • giving money to a candidate or a political party • doing any work to help a candidate in his or her race during the past two years	(Zhang et al., 2013)

Table 6A Most common measurement instruments for social media news use.

Number of items	Scale	Items	Used by
8		How often use the following social media platforms to get news? • Twitter • Facebook • Reddit • Google+ • LinkedIn • Tumblr • Instagram • Pinterest	(Saldaña et al., 2015)
3	1–7	How often do you use social media for the following activities? • getting/posting news • information • engaging in current events and public issues	(Kim & Chen, 2015)
3	1–5	How often do you use social media such as Twitter or Facebook for the following activities? • to get updates about the community • to share news about politics and society • to get tips on political news and events	(Stromback et al., 2018)
1	1–4	How often use the following social media platforms to get news? • Facebook • Twitter • Country-specific examples were included in the questionnaire	(Ahmed & Cho, 2019)

Table 7A Most common measurement instruments for incidental news exposure.

Number of items	Scale	Items	Used by
3		How much do you agree with the following statements? • stumble across news only by accident • only see political posts when other people from their network post about politics, and • do not seek political information, but sometimes see political information by accident	(Heiss et al., 2020)
1	1–7	How often are you accidentally exposed to political posts in your social media newsfeed without having actively searched for or intentionally included such information in your newsfeed (e.g., by "liking" news sources or politicians)?	(Heiss & Matthes, 2019)
3	1–4	When you use social networks/social media platforms (e.g., Facebook, Twitter, YouTube, etc.) how often do you come across news and information on the following when you may have been going online for a purpose other than to get the news? • current events • public issues • politics	(Lee & Xenos, 2020)

Table 8A Most common measurement instruments for second/dual screening.

Number of items	Scale	Items	Used by
3	1–5	Over the last two months, how often did you use social networks/social media platforms to read about and discuss televised news programs while aired? • during news programs • during campaign speeches, interviews, or debates involving politicians • during news coverage of the elections	(Vaccari & Valeriani, 2018b)
3		How often do you engage in dual screening while watching TV programs about the following topics? • political speeches or debates • news and public affairs • information about "election coverage"	(Gil de Zúñiga & Liu, 2017)
4	1–5	Four items measuring dual-screening use were self-generated when asking the extent to use various social media platforms (e.g., mobile instant messaging and social networking sites, such as Facebook, Weibo, and Instagram; video and TV sites/apps) while viewing current affair-related videos on two screen devices.	(Lin, 2019)

Table 9A Most common measurement instruments for political discussion.

Number of items	Scale	Items	Used by
7	1–7	Through seven items, participants rated how often during the last year they had joined online political discussions (e.g., joining political discussion through Facebook or Twitter)	(Alberici & Milesi, 2018)
9		How frequently do you engage in discussions about politics and public affairs with the following people? • spouse or partner • family and relatives • friends • acquaintances • strangers • neighbors you know very well • neighbors you do not know well • co-workers you know well • co-workers you do not know well	(Gil de Zúñiga, Diehl, et al., 2017)

Table 10A Most common measurement instruments for political discussion heterogeneity.

Number of items	Scale	Items	Used by
3	1–7	How often do you talk about social or public issues on social media with the following? • people who do not share their age, socio-economic status, or gender • people who disagree with their views • people who agree with their views	(Kim & Chen, 2015)
4	1–10	How often do you talk about politics or public affairs online and offline with the following? • people who disagree • people with different political views • people from different race or ethnicity • people from different social class	(Yoo & Gil de Zúñiga, 2019)
3		Who would you include as Facebook friends? • only acquaintances • people whom one has met only once or twice • even strangers How would you describe your Facebook friends? • Most of them are of similar background.	(Tang & Lee, 2013)

Table 10A (cont.)

Number of items	Scale	Items	Used by
		• Many of them are from different backgrounds, but still a significant portion are from similar background.	
		• They come from a variety of backgrounds.	
		How many of your Facebook friends are of a similar age?	
		• 0–20%	
		• 21–40%	
		• 41–60%	
		• 61–80%	
		• 81–100%	

Table 11A Most common measurement instruments for political discussion network size.

Number of items	Items	Used by
1	What is the rough number of friends linked to your Facebook account?	(Tang & Lee, 2013)
1	What is the size of your political discussion network on Facebook?	(Cao, 2020)
1	The size of an individual’s online social network is measured along a six-point scale according to respondents’ estimates of how many “people are on your list of ‘followers,’ ‘friends,’ ‘connections,’ or contacts” on the SNS that they use most often.	(Kahne & Bowyer, 2018)
2	With how many people did you talk about politics or public affairs during the past month in the following settings? • face-to-face or on the phone • via the internet (including chat rooms and social networking sites)	(Gil de Zúñiga, Diehl, et al., 2017)

Table 12A Most common measurement instruments for social media political expression.

Number of items	Scale	Items	Used by
14	1–6	How frequently did you perform one of the following behaviors (in regards to political content) on the four platforms listed below? • Facebook: 5 items • Twitter: 7 items • Snapchat: 1 item • Instagram: 1 item • sharing • liking • tweeting • etc.	(Kwak et al., 2018)
5		How often do you use social networking sites to do the following? • posting personal experiences related to politics or campaigning • friending a political advocate or politician • posting or sharing thoughts about politics • posting or sharing photos, videos, or audio files about politics • forwarding someone else's political commentary to other people	(Gil de Zúñiga, Molyneux, et al., 2014)
1	0–4	How often have you participated in a campaign that involved changing your profile picture?	(Chapman & Coffé, 2016)
2		How often do you share information on social media about the following? • social issues • political issues	(Chan et al., 2017)

Table 13A Most common measurement instruments for general social media use.

Number of items	Scale	Items	Used by
6	1–10	• On a typical day, how much time do you spend on online social networking sites? • How much do you use the Internet for social networking? To what extent do social networking sites help you to do the following? • stay in touch with family and friends • meet people who share my interests • stay informed about my local community • get news about current events through family and friends	(Gil de Zúñiga, Copeland, et al., 2014a)
4	1–5	What is your level of use for the following? • Facebook • Twitter • Instagram • blogs	(Mustapha & Omar, 2020)

Social Media and Political Knowledge

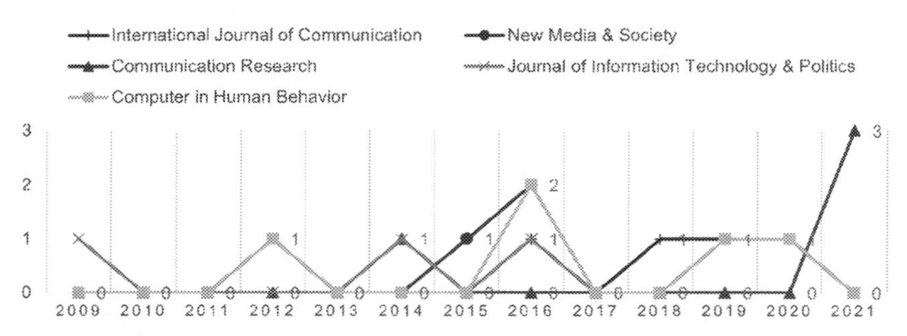

Figure 6A Number of publications in the top five journals with most published articles by year.

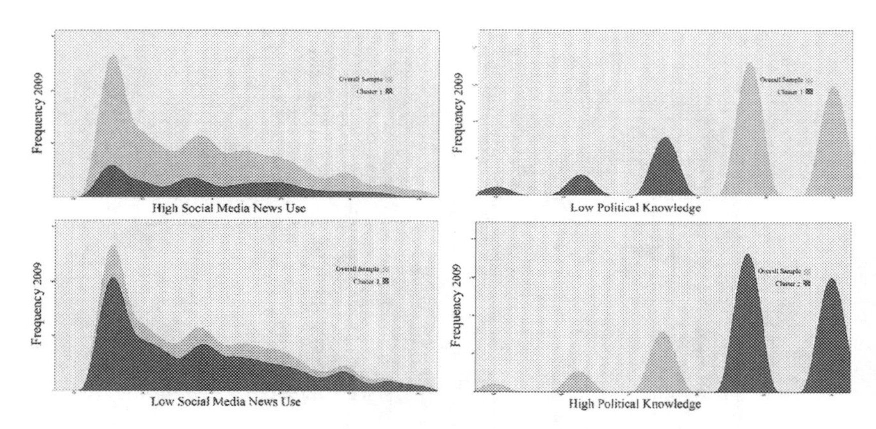

Figure 7A K-Means cluster algorithm data distributions for social media news use and political knowledge in 2009.

Note. The data visualization compares 2009 Overall Sample of Social Media News Use and Political Knowledge Distributions within the two clusters. Top figures correspond to Cluster 1: High Social Media Use and Low Political Knowledge. Bottom figures represent Cluster 2: Low Social Media News Use and High Political Knowledge.

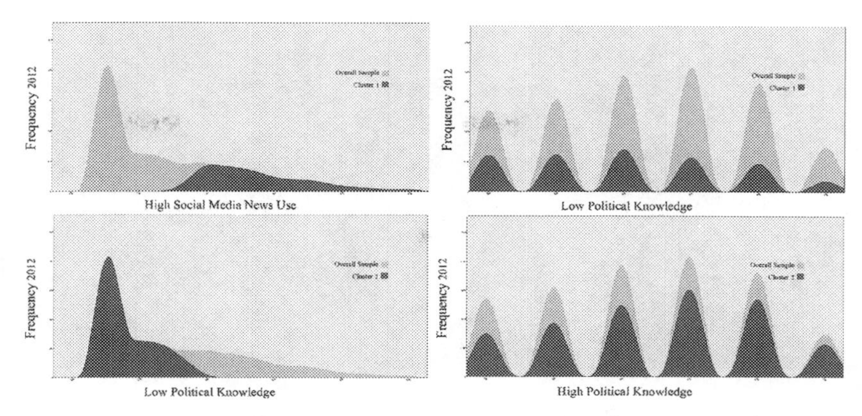

Figure 8A K-Means cluster algorithm data distributions for social media news use and political knowledge in 2013.

Note. The data visualization compares 2013 Overall Sample of Social Media News Use and Political Knowledge Distributions within the two clusters. Top figures correspond to Cluster 1: High Social Media Use and High Political Knowledge. Bottom figures represent Cluster 2: Low Social Media News Use and Low Political Knowledge.

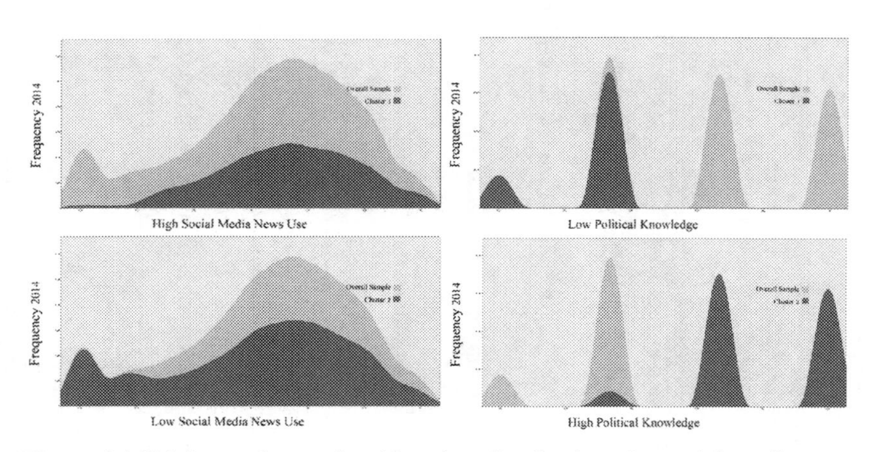

Figure 9A K-Means cluster algorithm data distributions for social media news use and political knowledge in 2015.

Note. The data visualization compares 2015 Overall Sample of Social Media News Use and Political Knowledge Distributions within the two clusters. Top figures correspond to Cluster 1: High Social Media Use and High Political Knowledge. Bottom figures represent Cluster 2: Low Social Media News Use and Low Political Knowledge.

Table 14A Most common measurement instruments for political social media use.

Number of items	Scale	Items	Used by
3		How often do you engage in the following behaviors on Facebook? • sharing or commenting political opinions on Facebook timelines of friends or other private citizens • liking or joining an institutionalized or noninstitutionalized Facebook group for a political or societal cause • creating a group for a political or societal cause	(Vissers & Stolle, 2014a)
3		Have you engaged in the following activities? • joined political, public, or citizen-led causes on social network sites in the past twelve months • joined groups or pages on Facebook related to the HidroAysén project • joined groups or pages on Facebook related to the student movement	(Valenzuela, 2013)
6	1–5	How often did you use social media for the following activities in the past twelve months? • participating in polls or voting • watching videos, seeing pictures, or listening to music • reading political news and posting replies to it • expressing political opinions • sharing and reposting others' posts • encouraging others to vote	(Choi & Kwon, 2019)

Table 15A List of journals for social media and political knowledge papers.

Journal	Number of articles
New Media & Society	6
Journal of Information Technology & Politics	5
Computer in Human Behavior	5
International Journal of Communication	4
Communication Research	4
Mass Communication and Society	4
Digital Journalism; *Political Communication*	3
American Behavioral Scientist; *Asian Journal of Communication*; *Communication Studies*; *Cyberpsychology Behavior and Social Networking*; *Journal of Broadcasting & Electronic Media*; *Journal of Computer-Mediated Communication*; *Journal of Youth Studies*; *Journalism and Mass Communication Quarterly*; *Malaysian Journal of Communication*	3
African Journalism Studies; *Atlantic Journal of Communication*; *Canadian Journal of Communication*; *Chinese Journal of Communication*; *Communication & Society*; *Communication-South African Journal for Communication Theory and Research*; *Conference Papers – American Political Science Association*; *Conference Papers – Southern Political Science Association*; *Educational Technology Research & Development*; *European Journal of Communication*; *Global Journal of Social Science*; *Information Communication & Society*; *Information Polity;* *Journal of Asian Pacific Communication*; *Journal of Communication*; *Journal of Contemporary African Studies*; *Journal of Current Issues and Research in Advertising*; *Mediterranean Politics*; *PLoS ONE*; *Science Computer Review*; *SEARCH: Journal of the Southeast Asia Research Centre for Communications and Humanities*; *Social Work (United States)*; *The Journal of Social Psychology*	1

Table 16A List of first author's country of origin for social media and political knowledge papers.

First author's country of origin	Number of papers
USA	38
Austria	6
Hong Kong	4
Netherlands	3
Belgium; Nigeria; Sweden	2
Canada; Chile; Denmark; Germany; Ghana; Indonesia; Iran; Israel; Italy; Kenya; Malaysia; New Zealand; Philippines; Singapore; Switzerland; Turkey; UK; Zimbabwe	1

Table 17A List of countries of data collection for social media and political knowledge papers.

Country	Number of papers
USA	37
Sweden	3
China; Multi-country; South Korea	3
Austria; Belgium; Denmark; Germany; Indonesia; Nigeria	2
Chile; Ghana; Hong Kong; Iran; Israel; Italy; Kenya; Netherlands; not specified; Philippines; Singapore; Taiwan; Turkey; Zimbabwe	1

Table 18A Most common measurement instruments for political knowledge.

Number of items	Details	Items	Used by
3	These analyses treated participants who answered two or three items correctly (60 percent of participants) as "high knowledge" and those who gave fewer than two correct answers as "low knowledge."	We assessed political knowledge by asking respondents three factual questions about the American political system.	(Bowyer & Kahn, 2019)
8		The political knowledge variable was measured by asking respondents questions with factually correct answers about the people, institutions, and processes of American government	(Barnidge et al., 2018)
		Respondents were asked factual knowledge questions about recent events that caught significant (social) media attention. Questions focused on political-economic issues.	(Boukes, 2019)
5	Answers were recoded such that correct responses were coded as 1 and incorrect responses were coded as 0.	Political knowledge was measured through a series of multiple-choice items dealing with a respondent's knowledge of the major political parties, governmental positions, and the rules of political processes	(Cacciatore et al., 2018)

Table 18A (cont.)

Number of items	Details	Items	Used by
3	For each question, respondents were asked to choose one of four possible answers or to indicate "Don't know." The answers were recoded (0 = incorrect or "Don't know," 1 = correct) and averaged.	Respondents' political knowledge was measured by using the following three factual questions that applied across all countries investigated: • Do you happen to know who the current Secretary-General of the United Nations is? • What international organization is in charge of monitoring the use of nuclear energy throughout the world? • You might have heard some people talking about global warming. In your mind, global warming is . . .	(Gil de Zúñiga et al., 2020)
8	Correct responses were coded as 1, while incorrect or missing ones were coded as 0.	This study assessed individuals' awareness of current events and knowledge about the overall functioning of the political system.	(Gil de Zúñiga et al., 2018)
10	Each question had a time limit of twenty seconds. If a response was not entered at the end of the twenty-second window, the survey proceeded to the	These questions pertained to news/political issues.	(Hopp et al., 2020)

	next question. Each question had five response categories, including a "Don't know" option. None of the questions were forced response. Responses were coded as: 0 = correct answer not provided, and 1 = correct answer.		
3	A "Don't know" option was included. Incorrect answers or those left blank were coded as 0 and correct answers were coded as 1.	Respondents indicated which candidate, Hillary Clinton or Donald Trump, was more in favor of the following policies: • raising the minimum wage • keeping the Affordable Care Act • getting rid of the nuclear deal with Iran	(Kanihan et al., 2020)
12	Respondents were asked to answer the questions to the best of their ability, without looking up the correct information, and quiz responses were timed. Correct answers were summed for a news knowledge score of 0–12.	Twelve multiple-choice questions about national and international events that are being discussed in the US news media at the time, including questions such as: • What does the term 'Common Core' refer to? • On which of these activities does the US government currently spend the most money? • Who is the current Prime Minister of Israel?	(Oeldorf-Hirsch, 2018)

Table 19A Most common measurement instruments for social media news use.

Number of items	Scale	Items	Used by
8		How often use the following social media platforms to get news? • Twitter • Facebook • Reddit • Google+ • LinkedIn • Tumblr • Instagram • Pinterest	(Saldaña et al., 2015)
2	1–7	How often during the past month did you engage or not in any of the following activities? • read political news links from friends and family • read political news links from news organizations or individual journalists they follow or subscribe to • read political news links from other organizations or public figures they follow or subscribe to	(Park & Kaye, 2019)
2	1–5	How often did you consume news on the following platforms in the past week? • Facebook • Twitter	(Edgerly et al., 2018)

Table 20A Most common measurement instruments for political discussion network size.

Number of items	Items	Used by
1	How many Facebook friends do you have?	(Cacciatore et al., 2018)
1	What is the sum of the network size on your two most frequently used social media sites?	(Li et al., 2016)

Table 21A Most common measurement instruments for political expression.

Number of items	Scale	Items	Used by
6	1–5	How often do you post about politics and the election on social media to do the following? • to express my political view • to criticize the political views I oppose • to raise awareness about a political issue or candidate • to provide information about a political issue or a candidate • to let people know that I am politically aware • to talk with others on social media about politics	(Kim et al., 2020)
8	1–10	How often do you engage in the following activities? • take part in posting personal experiences related to politics or campaigning • take part in posting or sharing thoughts about current events or politics • take part in posting or sharing photos, videos, memes, or gifs created by others that relate to current events or politics • take part in forwarding someone else's political commentary to other people • post [their] thoughts about current events or politics • post [their] experiences related to politics or campaigning	(Barnidge et al., 2018)

		• take part in posting or sharing photos, videos, memes, or gifs created by [them] that relate to current events or politics • created posts for [their] own blog about current events or public affairs	
5	1–5	How often do you engage in the following activites? • send messages about political campaigns • criticize government policy or action • make fun of the government policy or action • interact with the government official accounts • discuss government policy or action	(Chen & Chan, 2017)

Table 22A Most common measurement instruments for general social media use.

Number of items	Scale	Items	Used by
2	0–7	How often do you make use of the following social media? • Twitter • Facebook	(Boukes, 2019)
1	0–1	Do you ever use social networking sites such as Twitter or Facebook?	(Gottfried et al., 2017)
3	1–5	During the last two weeks, how often did you use the following three types of social media? • Facebook • Twitter • Youtube	(Park, 2019)
4	0–7	How often do you use the following social media platforms? • Facebook • Twitter • Youtube • Instagram	(Lee, 2019)
1	0–6	How often do you use Facebook?	(Lee & Xenos, 2019)

References

Abdulla, R., Poell, T., Rieder, B., Woltering, R., & Zack, L. (2018). Facebook polls as proto-democratic instruments in the Egyptian revolution: The 'We Are All Khaled Said' Facebook page. *Global Media and Communication*, 14(1), 141–160. https://doi.org/10.1177/1742766518760085

Ahmad, T., Alvi, A., & Ittefaq, M. (2019). The use of social media on political participation among university students: An analysis of survey results from rural Pakistan. *SAGE Open*, 9(3). https://doi.org/10.1177/2158244019864484

Ahmed, S., & Cho, J. (2019). The roles of different news media use and press freedom in education generated participation inequality: An eight country comparative analysis. *Journal of Broadcasting & Electronic Media*, 63(3), 566–586. https://doi.org/10.1080/08838151.2019.1653100

Ahmed, Y. A., Ahmad, M. N., Ahmad, N., & Zakaria, N. H. (2019). Social media for knowledge-sharing: A systematic literature review. *Telematics and Informatics*, 37, 72–112. https://doi.org/10.1016/j.tele.2018.01.015

Akkor, E. H. (2017). The role of social media as a negotiation sphere for 'public good': The case North Cyprus. *Revista de Cercetare si Interventie Sociala*, 59 (December), 86–103.

Alam, A., Adnan, H. M., & Kotamjani, S. S. (2019). Examining the impact of using social networks on political knowledge and political attitude by Iranian university students. *Jurnal Komunikasi – Malaysian Journal of Communication*, 35(3), 125–140. https://doi.org/10.17576/JKMJC-2019-3503-08

Alberici, A. I., & Milesi, P. (2018). Online discussion and the moral pathway to identity politicization and collective action. *Europe's Journal of Psychology*, 14(1), 143–158. https://doi.org/10.5964/ejop.v14i1.1507

Allcott, H., & Gentzkow, M. (2017). Social media and fake news in the 2016 election. *Journal of Economic Perspectives*, 31(2), 211–236. https://doi.org/10.1257/jep.31.2.211

Amaral, I., Zamora, R., Grandío, M. del M., & Noguera, J. M. (2016). Flows of communication and 'influentials' in Twitter: A comparative approach between Portugal and Spain during 2014 European elections. *Observatorio (OBS*)*, 10(2), 111–128. https://doi.org/10.15847/obsOBS1022016900

American Association of Public Opinion Research (2008). Standard definitions: Final dispositions of case codes and outcome rates for surveys. AAPOR. www.aapor.org/uploads/Standard_Definitions_04_08_Final.pdf

American Association of Public Opinion Research (2011). Standard definitions: Final dispositions of case codes and outcome rates for surveys. AAPOR. www.aapor.org/Standards-Ethics/Standard-Definitions-(1).aspx

American Association of Public Opinion Research (2016). Standard definitions: Final dispositions of case codes and outcome rates for surveys. AAPOR. www.aapor.org/AAPOR_Main/media/publications/Standard-Definitions 20169theditionfinal.pdf

Amsalem, E., & Zoizner, A. (2023). Do people learn about politics on social media? A meta-analysis of 76 studies. *Journal of Communication*, 73(1), 3–13. https://doi.org/10.1093/joc/jqac034

Andersen, R., Tilley, J., & Heath, A. F. (2005). Political knowledge and enlightened preferences: Party choice through the electoral cycle. *British Journal of Political Science*, 35(2), 285–302. https://doi.org/10.1017/S0007123405000153

Andı, S., Aytaç, S. E., & Çarkoğlu, A. (2020). Internet and social media use and political knowledge: Evidence from Turkey. *Mediterranean Politics*, 25(5), 579–599.

Arnold, J. R. (2012). The electoral consequences of voter ignorance. *Electoral Studies*, 31(4), 796–815. https://doi.org/10.1016/j.electstud.2012.06.003

Aronson, E. (1999). The power of self-persuasion. *American Psychologist*, 54(11), 875–884.

Astuti, P. A. A., & Hangsing, P. (2018). Predicting the behavior of young voters in elections: A case study of governor election in Jakarta, Indonesia. *Jurnal Komunikasi – Malaysian Journal of Communication*, 34(4), 357–372. https://doi.org/10.17576/JKMJC-2018-3404-21

Barnidge, M., Ardèvol-Abreu, A., & Zúñiga, H. G. (2018). Content-expressive behavior and ideological extremity: An examination of the roles of emotional intelligence and information network heterogeneity. *New Media & Society*, 20(2), 815–834.

Bartels, L. M. (1996). Uninformed votes: Information effects in presidential elections. *Journal of Political Science*, 40(1), 194–230.

Beam, M. A., Hutchens, M. J., & Hmielowski, J. D. (2016). Clicking vs. sharing: The relationship between online news behaviors and political knowledge. *Computers in Human Behavior*, 59, 215–220.

Beckers, K., Van Aelst, P., Verhoest, P., & D'Haenens, L. (2020). What do people learn from following the news? A diary study on the influence of media use on knowledge of current news stories. *European Journal of Communication*, 0267323120978724. https://doi.org/10.1177/0267323120978724

Bimber, B., & Copeland, L. (2013). Digital media and traditional political participation over time in the US. *Journal of Information Technology and Politics*, 10(2), 125–137. https://doi.org/10.1080/19331681.2013.769925

Birdwell, J., Feve, S., Tryhorn, C., & Vibla, N. (2013). Democracy in Europe can no longer be taken for granted… Backsliders Executive Summary. London: Demos.

Blais, A., Gidengil, E., Nevitte, N., & Nadeau, R. (2004). Where does turnout decline come from? *European Journal of Political Research*, 43(2), 221–236. https://doi.org/10.1111/j.1475-6765.2004.00152.x

Bode, L. (2016). Political news in the news feed: Learning politics from social media. *Mass Communication and Society*, 19(1), 24–48. https://doi.org/10.1080/15205436.2015.1045149

Bode, L. (2017). Closing the gap: Gender parity in political engagement on social media. *Information Communication and Society*, 20(4), 587–603. https://doi.org/10.1080/1369118X.2016.1202302

Bode, L., & Dalrymple, K. E. (2016). Politics in 140 characters or less: Campaign communication, network interaction, and political participation on Twitter. *Journal of Political Marketing*, 15(4), 311–332. https://doi.org/10.1080/15377857.2014.959686

Bond, R. M., Fariss, C. J., Jones, J. J., Kramer, A. D. I., Marlow, C., Settle, J. E., & Fowler, J. H. (2012). A 61-million-person experiment in social influence and political mobilization. *Nature*, 489(7415), 295–298. https://doi.org/10.1038/nature11421

Boukes, M. (2019). Social network sites and acquiring current affairs knowledge: The impact of Twitter and Facebook usage on learning about the news. *Journal of Information Technology & Politics*, 16(1), 36–51.

Boulianne, S. (2020). Twenty years of digital media effects on civic and political participation. *Communication Research*, 47(7), 947–966.

Bowyer, B., & Kahn, J. (2019). Motivated circulation: How misinformation and ideological alignment influence the circulation of political content. *International Journal of Communication*, 13, 5791–5815.

Boyd, D. (2010). Social network sites as networked publics: Affordances, dynamics, and implications. In A networked self: Identity, community, and culture on social network sites (ed. Z. Papacharissi), pp. 47–66. Routledge: New York.

Brady, H. E., Verba, S., & Schlozman, K. L. (1995). Beyond SES: A resource model of political participation. *American Political Science Review*, 89(2), 271–294.

Buente, W. (2015). Relating digital citizenship to informed citizenship online in the 2008 U.S. presidential election. *Information Polity*, 20(4), 269–285. https://doi.org/10.3233/IP-150375

Bulger, M., & Davison, & P. (2018). The promises, challenges, and futures of media literacy. *Journal of Media Literacy Education*, 10(1), 1–21.

Cacciatore, M. A., Yeo, S. K., Scheufele, D. A., Xenos, M. A., Brossard, D., & Corley, E. A. (2018). Is Facebook making us dumber? Exploring social media use as a predictor of political knowledge. *Journalism & Mass Communication Quarterly*, 95(2), 404–424.

Cao, X. (2020). Revisiting the democratic implications of political discussion disagreement: With whom one disagrees matters. *Journal of Information Technology & Politics*, 17(3), 193–207.

Castells, M. (2007). Communication, power and counter-power in the network society. *International Journal of Communication*, 1(1), 238–266.

Castells, M. (2009). The rise of the network society, Volume 1. John Wiley & Sons: Chichester.

Chaffee, S. H., & Kanihan, S. F. (1997). Learning about politics from the mass media. *Political Communication*, 14(4), 421–430. https://doi.org/10.1080/105846097199218

Chan, M., Chen, H.-T., & Lee, F. L. F. (2017). Examining the roles of mobile and social media in political participation: A cross-national analysis of three Asian societies using a communication mediation approach. *New Media & Society*, 19(12), 2003–2021. https://doi.org/10.1177/1461444816653190

Chapman, H., & Coffé, H. (2016). Changing Facebook profile pictures as part of a campaign: Who does it and why? *Journal of Youth Studies*, 19(4), 483–500. https://doi.org/10.1080/13676261.2015.1083962

Chen, Z., & Chan, M. (2017). Motivations for social media use and impact on political participation in China: A cognitive and communication mediation approach. *CyberPsychology, Behavior & Social Networking*, 20(2), 83–90.

Choi, Y.-T., & Kwon, G.-H. (2019). New forms of citizen participation using SNS: An empirical approach. *Quality and Quantity*, 53(1), 1–17. https://doi.org/10.1007/s11135-018-0720-y

Chon, M.-G., & Park, H. (2020). Social media activism in the digital age: Testing an integrative model of activism on contentious issues. *Journalism & Mass Communication Quarterly*, 97(1), 72–97. https://doi.org/10.1177/1077699019835896

Christin, T., Hug, S., & Sciarini, P. (2002). Interests and information in referendum voting: An analysis of Swiss voters. *European Journal of Political Research*, 41(6), 759–776. https://doi.org/10.1111/1475-6765.t01-1-00030

Christofides, E., Muise, A., & Desmarais, S. (2009). Information disclosure and control on Facebook: Are they two sides of the same coin or two different processes? *Cyberpsychology & Behavior*, 12(3), 341–345.

Chunly, S. (2019). Facebook and political participation in Cambodia: Determinants and impact of online political behaviours in an authoritarian state. *South East Asia Research*, 27(4), 378–397. https://doi.org/10.1080/0967828X.2019.1692635

Chwe, M. S. Y. (1999). Structure and strategy in collective action. *American Journal of Sociology*, 105(1), 128–156. https://doi.org/10.1086/210269

Clarke, K., & Kocak, K. (2020). Launching revolution: Social media and the Egyptian uprising's first movers. *British Journal of Political Science*, 50(3), 1025–1045. https://doi.org/10.1017/S0007123418000194

Cogburn, D. L., & Espinoza-Vasquez, F. K. (2011). From networked nominee to networked nation: Examining the impact of web 2.0 and social media on political participation and civic engagement in the 2008 Obama campaign. *Journal of Political Marketing*, 10(1–2), 189–213. https://doi.org/10.1080/15377857.2011.540224

Conway, M. M. (1985). Political participation in the United States. Congressional Quarterly: Washington, DC.

Costanza-Chock, S. (2012). Mic check! Media cultures and the Occupy movement. *Social Movement Studies*, 11(3–4), 375–385. https://doi.org/10.1080/14742837.2012.710746

Cox, J. M. (2017). *The source of a movement: Making the case for social media as an informational source using Black Lives Matter.* Ethnic and Racial Studies, 40(11), 1847–1854. https://doi.org/10.1080/01419870.2017.1334935

Da Silva Nogueira, D., & Papageorgiou, M. M. (2020). Standing still or ascending in the social media political participation ladder? Evidence from Iran. *Revista Espanola de Ciencia Politica*, 2020(53), 13–29. https://doi.org/10.21308/recp.53.01

David, C. C., San Pascual, M. R. S., & Torres, M. E. S. (2019). Reliance on Facebook for news and its influence on political engagement. *PLoS ONE*, 14(3), 1–15.

De Tocqueville, A. (1863). Democracy in America. Sever and Francis: Cambridge, MA.

Delli Carpini, M. X., & Keeter, S. (1993). Measuring political knowledge: Putting first things first. *American Journal of Political Science*, 37(4), 1179–1206.

Delli Carpini, M. X., & Keeter, S. (1996). What Americans know about politics and why it matters. Yale University Press: New Haven, CT.

Dey, S. (2020). Let there be clamor: Exploring the emergence of a new public sphere in India and use of social media as an instrument of activism. *Journal of Communication Inquiry*, 44(1), 48–68. https://doi.org/10.1177/0196859919827319

Diehl, T., Barnidge, M., & Zúñiga, H. (2019). Multi-platform news use and political participation across age groups: Toward a valid metric of platform diversity and its effects. *Journalism and Mass Communication Quarterly*, 96(2), 428–451. https://doi.org/10.1177/1077699018783960

Edgerly, S., Thorson, K., & Wells, C. (2018). Young citizens, social media, and the dynamics of political learning in the U.S. Presidential Primary Election. *American Behavioral Scientist*, 62(8), 1042–1060.

Ekström, M., & Östman, J. (2015). Information, interaction, and creative production: The effects of three forms of internet use on youth democratic engagement. *Communication Research*, 42(6), 796–818. https://doi.org/10.1177/0093650213476295

Erkel, P. F. A., & Van Aelst, P. (2020). Why don't we learn from social media? Studying effects of and mechanisms behind social media news use on general surveillance political knowledge. *Political Communication*, 38(4), 407–425. https://doi.org/10.1080/10584609.2020.1784328

Estabrook, R., & Neale, M. (2013). A comparison of factor score estimation methods in the presence of missing data: Reliability and an application to nicotine dependence. *Multivariate Behavioral Research*, 48(1), 1–27.

Eveland, J. (2004). The effect of political discussion in producing informed citizens: The roles of information, motivation, and elaboration. *Political Communication*, 21(2), 177–193.

Eveland, W. P. (2002). News information processing as mediator of the relationship between motivations and political knowledge. *Journalism & Mass Communication Quarterly*, 79(1), 26–40. https://doi.org/10.1177/107769900207900103

Eveland, W. P., Jr, & Thomson, T. (2006). Is it talking, thinking, or both? A lagged dependent variable model of discussion effects on political knowledge. *Journal of Communication*, 56(3), 523–542. https://doi.org/10.1111/j.1460-2466.2006.00299.x

Faria, C., & Rehbein, M. (2016). Open parliament policy applied to the Brazilian Chamber of Deputies. *The Journal of Legislative Studies*, 22(4), 559–578. https://doi.org/10.1080/13572334.2016.1235333

Feezell, J. T., Conroy, M., & Guerrero, M. (2009). Facebook is . . . fostering political engagement: A study of online social networking groups and offline participation. APSA 2009 Toronto Meeting Paper. SSRN. https://ssrn.com/abstract=1451456

Feezell, J. T., & Ortiz, B. (2019). I saw it on Facebook": An experimental analysis of political learning through social media. *Information Communication & Society*, 24(9), 1283–1302. https://doi.org/10.1080/1369118X.2019.1697340

Fowler, A., & Margolis, M. (2014). The political consequences of uninformed voters. *Electoral Studies*, 34, 100–110. https://doi.org/10.1016/j.electstud.2013.09.009

Gainous, J., Abbott, J. P., & Wagner, K. M. (2020). Active vs. passive social media engagement with critical information: Protest behavior in two asian countries. *International Journal of Press-Politics*, 26(2), 464–483. https://doi.org/10.1177/1940161220963606

Gallego, A. (2009). Where else does turnout decline come from? Education, age, generation and period effects in three european countries. *Scandinavian Political Studies*, 32(1), 23–44. https://doi.org/10.1111/j.1467-9477.2008.00212.x

Galston, W. A. (2001). Political knowledge, political engagement, and civic education. *Annual Review of Political Science*, 4(1), 217–234.

Garcia-Castañon, M., Rank, A. D., & Barreto, M. A. (2011). Plugged in or tuned out? Youth, race, and internet usage in the 2008 election. *Journal of Political Marketing*, 10(1–2), 115–138. https://doi.org/10.1080/15377857.2011.540209

Garrido, M. V., Zentner, A., & Busse, R. (2011). The effects of gatekeeping: A systematic review of the literature. *Scandinavian Journal of Primary Health Care*, 29(1), 28–38. https://doi.org/10.3109/02813432.2010.537015

Gerl, K., Marschall, S., & Wilker, N. (2018). Does the internet encourage political participation? Use of an online platform by members of a German political party. *Policy and Internet*, 10(1), 87–118. https://doi.org/10.1002/poi3.149

Gibson, R., & Cantijoch, M. (2013). Conceptualizing and measuring participation in the age of the internet: Is online political engagement really different to offline? *The Journal of Politics*, 75(3), 701–716. https://doi.org/10.1017/S0022381613000431

Giglietto, F., & Selva, D. (2014). Second screen and participation: A content analysis on a full season dataset of tweets. *Journal of Communication*, 64(2), 260–277. https://doi.org/10.1111/jcom.12085

Gil de Zúñiga, H. (2012). Social media use for news and individuals' social capital: Civic engagement and political participation. *Journal of Computer-Mediated Communication*, 17(3), 319–336. https://doi.org/10.1111/j.1083-6101.2012.01574.x

Gil de Zúñiga, H., Ardevol-Abreu, A., & Casero-Ripolles, A. (2019). WhatsApp political discussion, conventional participation and activism: Exploring direct, indirect and generational effects. *Information Communication & Society*, 24(2), 201–218. https://doi.org/10.1080/1369118X.2019.1642933

Gil de Zúñiga, H., Barnidge, M., & Scherman, A. (2017). Social media social Capital, offline social capital, and citizenship: Exploring asymmetrical social capital effects. *Political Communication*, 34(1), 44–68. https://doi.org/10.1080/10584609.2016.1227000

Gil de Zúñiga, H., Copeland, L., & Bimber, B. (2014a). Political consumerism: Civic engagement and the social media connection. *New Media & Society*, 16(3), 488–506. https://doi.org/10.1177/1461444813487960

Gil de Zúñiga, H., Copeland, L., & Bimber, B. (2014b). Political consumerism: Civic engagement and the social media connection. *New Media & Society*, 16(3), 488–506. https://doi.org/10.1177/1461444813487960

Gil de Zúñiga, H., & Diehl, T. (2019). News finds me perception and democracy: Effects on political knowledge, political interest, and voting. *New Media & Society*, 21(6), 1253–1271.

Gil de Zúñiga, H., Diehl, T., & Ardévol-Abreu, A. (2017). Internal, external, and government political efficacy: Effects on news use, discussion, and political participation. *Journal of Broadcasting & Electronic Media*, 61(3), 574–596. https://doi.org/10.1080/08838151.2017.1344672

Gil de Zúñiga, H., Diehl, T., & Ardèvol-Abreu, A. (2018). When citizens and journalists interact on Twitter: Expectations of journalists' performance on social media and perceptions of media bias. *Journalism Studies*, 19(2), 227–246.

Gil de Zúñiga, H., Garcia-Perdomo, V., & McGregor, S. C. (2015). What is second screening? Exploring motivations of second screen use and its effect on online political participation. *Journal of Communication*, 65(5), 793–815. https://doi.org/10.1111/jcom.12174

Gil de Zúñiga, H., González-González, P., & Goyanes, M. (2021). Pathways to political persuasion: Linking online, social media, and fake news with political attitude change through political discussion. *American Behavioral Scientist*, 0(0). https://doi.org/10.1177/00027642221118272

Gil de Zúñiga, H., & Liu, J. H. (2017). Second screening politics in the social media sphere: Advancing research on dual screen use in political communication with evidence from 20 countries. *Journal of Broadcasting & Electronic Media*, 61(2), 193–219. https://doi.org/10.1080/08838151.2017.1309420

Gil de Zúñiga, H., Molyneux, L., & Zheng, P. (2014). Social media, political expression, and political participation: Panel analysis of lagged and concurrent relationships. *Journal of Communication*, 64(4), 612–634. https://doi.org/10.1111/jcom.12103

Gil de Zúñiga, H., Scheffauer, R., & Zhang, B. (2023). Cable news Uue and conspiracy theories: Exploring Fox News, CNN, and MSNBC effects on people's conspiracy mentality. *Journalism & Mass Communication Quarterly*, 0(0). https://doi.org/10.1177/10776990231171929

Gil de Zúñiga, H., Strauss, N., & Huber, B. (2020). The proliferation of the "News Finds Me" Perception across societies. *International Journal of Communication*, 14, 1605–1633.

Gil de Zúñiga, H., & Valenzuela, S. (2011). The mediating path to a stronger citizenship: Online and offline networks, weak ties, and civic engagement. *Communication Research*, 38(3), 397–421. https://doi.org/10.1177/0093650210384984

Gil de Zúñiga, H., Veenstra, A., Vraga, E., & Shah, D. (2010). Digital democracy: Reimagining pathways to political participation. *Journal of Information Technology and Politics*, 7(1), 36–51. https://doi.org/10.1080/19331680903316742

Gil de Zúñiga, H., Weeks, B., & Ardèvol-Abreu, A. (2017). Effects of the News-Finds-Me Perception in communication: Social media use implications for news seeking and learning about politics. *Journal of Computer-Mediated Communication*, 22(3), 105–123.

Gilens, M. (2001). Political ignorance and collective policy preferences. *American Political Science Review*, 95(2), 379–396. https://doi.org/10.1017/S0003055401002222

Gomez, B. T., & Wilson, J. M. (2001). Political sophistication and economic voting in the American electorate: A theory of heterogeneous attribution. *American Journal of Political Science*, 45(4), 899–914. https://doi.org/10.2307/2669331

Gorokhovskaia, Y., Shahbaz, A., & Slipowitz, A. (2023). The Freedom House survey for 2022: A turning point for global freedom? *Journal of Democracy*, 34(2), 105–119.

Gottfried, J. A., Hardy, B. W., Holbert, R. L., Winneg, K. M., & Jamieson, K. H. (2017). The changing nature of political debate consumption: Social media, multitasking, and knowledge acquisition. *Political Communication*, 34(2), 172–199.

Goyanes, M., Ardèvol-Abreu, A., & Gil de Zúñiga, H. (2023). Antecedents of news avoidance: Competing effects of political interest, news overload, trust in news media, and "News Finds Me" Perception. *Digital Journalism*, 11(1), 1–18. https://doi.org/10.1080/21670811.2021.1990097

Graham, E. E., Tang, T., & Mahoney, L. M. (2020). Family matters: A functional model of family communication patterns and political participation. *Communication Studies*, 71(2), 262–279. https://doi.org/10.1080/10510974.2020.1726426

Granovetter, M. S. (1973). The strength of weak ties. *American Journal of Sociology*, 78, 1360–1380. https://doi.org/10.1016/B978-0-12-442450-0.50025-0

Grönlund, K., & Setälä, M. (2007). Political trust, satisfaction and voter turnout. *Comparative European Politics*, 5(4), 400–422. https://doi.org/10.1057/palgrave.cep.6110113

Großer, J., & Seebauer, M. (2016). The curse of uninformed voting: An experimental study. *Games and Economic Behavior*, 97, 205–226. https://doi.org/10.1016/j.geb.2016.04.009

Halpern, D., Valenzuela, S., & Katz, J. E. (2017). We face, I tweet: How different social media influence political participation through collective and internal efficacy. *Journal of Computer-Mediated Communication*, 22(6), 320–336. https://doi.org/10.1111/jcc4.12198

Hamanaka, S. (2020). The role of digital media in the 2011 Egyptian revolution. *Democratization*, 27(5), 777–796. https://doi.org/10.1080/13510347.2020.1737676

Hao, X., Wen, N., & George, C. (2014). News consumption and political and civic engagement among young people. *Journal of Youth Studies*, 17(9), 1221–1238.

Hargittai, E., & Hinnant, A. (2008). Digital inequality: Differences in young adults' use of the Internet. *Communication Research*, 35(5), 602–621. https://doi.org/10.1177/0093650208321782

Hargittai, E., & Shaw, A. (2013). Digitally savvy citizenship: The role of internet skills and engagement in young adults' political participation around the 2008 presidential election. *Journal of Broadcasting & Electronic Media*, 57(2), 115–134. https://doi.org/10.1080/08838151.2013.787079

Hassim, N., Zian, S. T. S., & Jayasainan, S. Y. (2020). The influence of peer engagement on voting among Malaysian youths through social networking sites. *SEARCH: Journal of the Southeast Asia Research Centre for Communications and Humanities*, 12(3), 125–144.

Heiss, R., Knoll, J., & Matthes, J. (2020). Pathways to political (dis-)engagement: Motivations behind social media use and the role of incidental and intentional exposure modes in adolescents' political engagement. *Communications: The European Journal of Communication Research*, 45, 671–693. https://doi.org/10.1515/commun-2019-2054

Heiss, R., & Matthes, J. (2019). Does incidental exposure on social media equalize or reinforce participatory gaps? Evidence from a panel study. *New Media & Society*, 21(11–12), 2463–2482. https://doi.org/10.1177/1461444819850755

Heiss, R., & Matthes, J. (2021). Funny cats and politics: Do humorous context posts impede or foster the elaboration of news posts on social media? *Communication Research*, 48(1), 100–124.

Hjorth, F., & Adler-Nissen, R. (2019). Ideological asymmetry in the reach of Pro-Russian digital disinformation to United States audiences. *Journal of Communication*, 69(2), 168–192.

Hobolt, S. B. (2007). Taking cues on Europe? Voter competence and party endorsements in referendums on European integration. *European Journal of Political Research*, 46, 151–182. https://doi.org/10.1111/j.1475-6765.2006.00688.x

Hoffman, L. H. (2012). Participation or communication? An explication of political activity in the internet age. *Journal of Information Technology and Politics*, 9(3), 217–233. https://doi.org/10.1080/19331681.2011.650929

Hoffmann, C. P., & Lutz, C. (2019). Digital divides in political participation: The mediating role of social media self-efficacy and privacy concerns. *Policy and Internet*, 10(2), 6–29. https://doi.org/10.1002/poi3.225

Hopp, T., Ferrucci, P., Vargo, C. J., & Fisher, J. (2020). Exposure to difference on Facebook, Ttust, and political knowledge. *Mass Communication & Society*, 23(6), 779–809.

Hosch-Dayican, B., Amrit, C., Aarts, K., & Dassen, A. (2016). How do online citizens persuade fellow voters? Using twitter during the 2012 Dutch parliamentary election campaign. *Social Science Computer Review*, 34(2), 135–152. https://doi.org/10.1177/0894439314558200

Housholder, E., & LaMarre, H. L. (2013). Political social media engagement: Comparing campaign goals with voter behavior. *Public Relations Review*, 41(1), 138–140. https://doi.org/10.1016/j.pubrev.2014.10.007

Houston, J. B., McKinney, M. S., Hawthorne, J., & Spialek, M. L. (2013). Frequency of tweeting during presidential debates: Effect on debate attitudes and knowledge. *Communication Studies*, 64(5), 548–560. https://doi.org/10.1080/10510974.2013.832693

Huckfeldt, R. R., & Sprague, J. (1995). Citizens, politics and social communication: Information and influence in an election campaign. Cambridge University Press: New York.

Janis, I. L., & King, B. T. (1954). The influence of role playing on opinion change. *The Journal of Abnormal and Social Psychology*, 49(2), 211–218. https://doi.org/10.1037/h0056957

Jennings, F. J. (2019). An uninformed electorate: Identity-motivated elaboration, partisan cues, and learning. *Journal of Applied Communication Research*, 47(5), 527–547. https://doi.org/10.1080/00909882.2019.1679385

Jennings, F. J., Coker, C. R., McKinney, M. S., & Warner, B. R. (2017). Tweeting presidential primary debates: Debate processing through motivated twitter instruction. *American Behavioral Scientist*, 61(4), 455–474.

Jensen, M. J. (2017). Social media and political campaigning: Changing terms of engagement? *International Journal of Press/Politics*, 22(1), 23–42. https://doi.org/10.1177/1940161216673196

Jiang, L. (2017). Why context matters: The role of campaign context in the relationship between digital media use and political participation. *Australian Journal of Political Science*, 52(4), 580–598. https://doi.org/10.1080/10361146.2017.1373064

Joia, L. A., & Soares, C. D. (2018). Social media and the trajectory of the "20 Cents Movement" in Brazil: An actor-network theory-based investigation. *Telematics and Informatics*, 35(8), 2201–2218. https://doi.org/10.1016/j.tele.2018.08.007

Jung, N., Kim, Y., & Zúñiga, H. G. (2011). The mediating role of knowledge and efficacy in the effects of communication on political participation. *Mass Communication and Society*, 14(4), 407–430. https://doi.org/10.1080/15205436.2010.496135

Kahne, J., & Bowyer, B. (2018). The political significance of social media activity and social networks. *Political Communication*, 35(3), 470–493. https://doi.org/10.1080/10584609.2018.1426662

Kamau, S. C. (2017). Democratic engagement in the digital age: Youth, social media and participatory politics in Kenya. *Communicatio: South African Journal for Communication Theory and Research*, 43(2), 128–146. https://doi.org/10.1080/02500167.2017.1327874

Kanihan, S. F., Meirick, P. C., & Segijn, C. M. (2020). Thinking, knowing, or thinking you know: The relationship between multiscreening and political learning. *Journalism & Mass Communication Quarterly*, 98(4), 1104–1128. https://doi.org/10.1177/1077699020960066

Kanihan, S. F., & Rim, H. (2018). Media use and political learning: Comparing Trump supporters to celebrity candidate voters. *Atlantic Journal of Communication*, 26(4), 251–266.

Karakaya, S., & Glazier, R. A. (2019). Media, information, and political participation: The importance of online news sources in the absence of a free press. *Journal of Information Technology and Politics*, 16(3), 290–306. https://doi.org/10.1080/19331681.2019.1645784

Kasadha, J. (2019). Does social media matter in developing democracies? Examining its impact on citizen political participation and expression in Uganda. *Journal of Public Affairs*, 20(1), e1981. https://doi.org/10.1002/pa.1981

Kim, D. H., Jones-Jang, S. M., & Kenski, K. (2020). Why do people share political information on social media? *Digital Journalism*, 9(8), 1123–1140. https://doi.org/10.1080/21670811.2020.1827966

Kim, Y., & Chen, H.-T. (2015). Discussion network heterogeneity matters: Examining a moderated mediation model of social media use and civic Engagement. *International Journal of Communication*, 9, 2344–2365.

Kim, Y., Chen, H.-T., & Wang, Y. (2016). Living in the smartphone age: Examining the conditional indirect effects of mobile phone use on political participation. *Journal of Broadcasting & Electronic Media*, 60(4), 694–713. https://doi.org/10.1080/08838151.2016.1203318

Kim, Y., Russo, S., & Amnå, E. (2017). The longitudinal relation between online and offline political participation among youth at two different developmental stages. *New Media & Society*, 19(6), 899–917. https://doi.org/10.1177/1461444815624181

Klašnja, M. (2017). Uninformed voters and corrupt politicians. *American Politics Research*, 45(2), 256–279. https://doi.org/10.1177/1532673X16684574

Kleinberg, M. S., & Lau, R. R. (2019). The importance of political knowledge for effective citizenship: Differences between the broadcast and internet generations. *Public Opinion Quarterly*, 83(2), 338–362.

Knobloch-Westerwick, S., & Meng, J. (2011). Reinforcement of the political self through selective exposure to political messages. *Journal of Communication*, 61(2), 349–368.

Ko, H.-C., & Kuo, F.-Y. (2009). Can blogging enhance subjective well-being through self-disclosure? *Cyberpsychology & Behavior*, 12(1), 75–79.

Kuklinski, J. H., & Quirk, P. J. (2000). Reconsidering the Rational Public: Cognition, Heuristics, and Mass Opinion. In Elements of reason: Cognition, choice, and the bounds of rationality (eds. A. Lupia, M. D. McCubbins, & S. L. Popkin), pp. 153–182. Cambridge University Press. https://doi.org/10.1017/CBO9780511805813.008

Kwak, N., Lane, D. S., Weeks, B. E., Kim, D. H., Lee, S. S., & Bachleda, S. (2018). Perceptions of social, edia for politics: Testing the slacktivism hypothesis. *Human Communication Research*, 44(2), 197–221. https://doi.org/10.1093/hcr/hqx008

Lane, D. S., Kim, D. H., Lee, S. S., Weeks, B. E., & Kwak, N. (2017). From online disagreement to offline action: How diverse motivations for using social media can increase political information sharing and catalyze offline political participation. *Social Media and Society*, 3(3), 1–14. https://doi.org/10.1177/2056305117716274

Larsson, A. O. (2020). Facebook as a "trusted space of everyday communication": Parties, citizens and direct representation. *Journal of Applied Journalism & Media Studies*, 9(2), 127–146. https://doi.org/10.1386/ajms_00019_1

Lee, C., Shin, J., & Hong, A. (2018). Does social media use really make people politically polarized? Direct and indirect effects of social media use on political polarization in South Korea. *Telematics and Informatics*, 35(1), 245–254. https://doi.org/10.1016/j.tele.2017.11.005

Lee, S. (2019). Connecting social media use with gaps in knowledge and participation in a protest context: The case of candle light vigil in South Korea. *Asian Journal of Communication*, 29(2), 111–127. https://doi.org/10.1080/01292986.2018.1549264

Lee, S. (2020). Probing the mechanisms through which social media erodes political knowledge: The role of the News-Finds-Me Perception. *Mass Communication & Society*, 23(6), 810–832.

Lee, S. W., Kim, I., Yoo, J., Park, S., Jeong, B., & Cha, M. (2016). Insights from an expressive writing intervention on Facebook to help alleviate depressive symptoms. *Computers in Human Behavior*, 62, 613–619.

Lee, S., & Xenos, M. (2019). Social distraction? Social media use and political knowledge in two U.S. Presidential Elections. *Computers in Human Behavior*, 90, 18–25.

Lee, S., & Xenos, M. (2020). Incidental news exposure via social media and political participation: Evidence of reciprocal effects. *New Media & Society*, 24(1), 178–201. https://doi.org/10.1177/1461444820962121

Lelkes, Y. (2020). A bigger pie: The effects of high-speed internet on political behavior. *Journal of Computer-Mediated Communication*, 25(3), 199–216. https://doi.org/10.1093/jcmc/zmaa002

Li, X., & Chan, M. (2017). Comparing social media use, discussion, political trust and political engagement among university students in China and Hong Kong: An application of the O–S–R–O–R model. *Asian Journal of Communication*, 27(1), 65–81. https://doi.org/10.1080/01292986.2016.1248454

Li, X., Lee, F. L. F., & Li, Y. (2016). The dual impact of social media under networked authoritarianism: Social media use, civic attitudes, and system support in China. *International Journal of Communication*, 10, 5143–5163.

Lijphart, A. (1997). Unequal participation: Democracy's unresolved dilemma presidential address, American Political Science Association, 1996. *American Political Science Review*, 91(1), 1–14. https://doi.org/10.2307/2952255

Likas, A., Vlassis, N., & J. Verbeek, J. (2003). The global k-means clustering algorithm. *Pattern Recognition*, 36(2), 451–461. https://doi.org/10.1016/S0031-3203(02)00060-2

Lin, C. A. (2009). Effects of the internet. In Media effects (eds. J. Bryant & M. B. Oliver), pp. 583–607. Routledge: New York.

Lin, T. T. C. (2019). Motivation and trust: How dual screening influences offline civic engagement among Taiwanese internet users. *International Journal of Communication*, 13, 4663–4681.

Lipsky, M. (1968). Protest as a political resource. *American Political Science Review*, 62(4), 1144–1158. https://doi.org/10.2307/1953909

Lu, Y. (2019). Incidental exposure to political disagreement on Facebook and corrective participation: Unraveling the effects of emotional responses and issue relevance. *International Journal of Communication*, 13, 874–896.

Maher, T. V., & Earl, J. (2019). Barrier or booster? Digital media, social networks, and youth micromobilization. *Sociological Perspectives*, 62(6), 865–883. https://doi.org/10.1177/0731121419867697

Maksl, A., Ashley, S., & Craft, S. (2015). Measuring news media literacy. *Journal of Media Literacy Education*, 6(3), 29–45. https://doi.org/10.23860/jmle-6-3-3

Manski, C. F. (1992). Income and higher education. *Focus*, 14(3), 14–19.

Martin, P. S. (2008). The mass media as sentinel: Why bad news about issues is good news for participation. *Political Communication*, 25(2), 180–193. https://doi.org/10.1080/10584600801985706

McLeod, J. M., Scheufele, D. A., & Moy, P. (1999). Community, communication, and participation: The role of mass media and interpersonal discussion in local political participation. *Political Communication*, 16(3), 315–336.

Michels, A., & de Graaf, L. (2010). Examining citizen participation: Local participatory policy making and democracy. *Local Government Studies*, 36(4), 477–491. https://doi.org/10.1080/03003930.2010.494101

Micó, J.-L., & Casero-Ripollés, A. (2014). Political activism online: Organization and media relations in the case of 15M in Spain. *Information, Communication & Society*, 17(7), 858–871. https://doi.org/10.1080/1369118X.2013.830634

Moffett, K. W., & Rice, L. L. (2018). College students and online political expression during the 2016 election. *Social Science Computer Review*, 36(4), 422–439. https://doi.org/10.1177/0894439317721186

Moher, D., Shamseer, L., Clarke, M., Ghersi, D., Liberati, A., Petticrew, M., Shekelle, P., Stewart, L. A., & PRISMA-P Group. (2015). Preferred reporting items for systematic review and meta-analysis protocols (PRISMA-P) 2015 statement. *Systematic Reviews*, 4(1), 1–9. https://doi.org/10.1186/2046-4053-4-1

Molaei, H. (2018). Justification and knowledge: Prospecting the modality of Indonesians' informal political discussions on Facebook. *Journal of Asian Pacific Communication*, 28(2), 323–344. https://doi.org/10.1075/japc.00015.mol

Moraes, G. H. S. M., Pelegrini, G. C., & Pinheiro, G. T. (2020). Social media and protests engagement: What's gender got to do with it? *Journal of Content, Community and Communication*, 10(6), 22–31. https://doi.org/10.31620/JCCC.06.20/03

Morris, D. S., & Morris, J. S. (2013). Digital inequality and participation in the political process: Real or Imagined? *Social Science Computer Review*, 31(5), 589–600. https://doi.org/10.1177/0894439313489259

Mundt, M., Ross, K., & Burnett, C. M. (2018). Scaling social movements through social media: The case of Black Lives Matter. *Social Media + Society*, 4(4), 1–14. https://doi.org/10.1177/2056305118807911

Mustapha, L. K., & Omar, B. (2020). Do social media matter? Examining social media use and youths' political participation during the 2019 Nigerian general elections. *Round Table*, 109(4), 441–457. https://doi.org/10.1080/00358533.2020.1788766

Mutahi, P., & Kimari, B. (2020). Fake news and the 2017 Kenyan elections. *Communicatio*, 46(4), 31–49. https://doi.org/10.1080/02500167.2020.1723662

Mwonzora, G. (2020). Social media and citizen mobilisation in the biometric voter registration (BVR) process in Zimbabwe. *Journal of Contemporary African Studies*, 38(1), 103–120.

Naab, T. K., & Sehl, A. (2017). Studies of user-generated content: A systematic review. *Journalism*, 18(10), 1256–1273. https://doi.org/10.1177/1464884916673557

Naderer, B., Heiss, R., & Matthes, J. (2020). The skilled and the interested: How personal curation skills increase or decrease exposure to political information on social media. *Journal of Information Technology & Politics*, 17(4), 452–460.

Nam, T. (2011). Whose e-democracy? The democratic divide in American electoral campaigns. *Information Polity*, 16(2), 131–150. https://doi.org/10.3233/IP-2011-0220

Nam, T., & Stromer-Galley, J. (2012). The democratic divide in the 2008 U.S. presidential election. *Journal of Information Technology and Politics*, 9(2), 133–149. https://doi.org/10.1080/19331681.2011.579858

Nanz, A., Heiss, R., & Matthes, J. (2020). Antecedents of intentional and incidental exposure modes on social media and consequences for political participation: A panel study. *Acta Politica*, 57, 235–253. https://doi.org/10.1057/s41269-020-00182-4

Oeldorf-Hirsch, A. (2018). The role of engagement in learning from active and incidental news exposure on social media. *Mass Communication and Society*, 21(2), 225–247. https://doi.org/10.1080/15205436.2017.1384022

Ohme, J. (2020). Mobile but not mobilized? Differential gains from mobile news consumption for citizens' political knowledge and campaign participation. *Digital Journalism*, 8(1), 103–125. https://doi.org/10.1080/21670811.2019.1697625

Osburn, H. G. (2000). Coefficient alpha and related internal consistency reliability coefficients. *Psychological Methods*, 5(3), 343–355.

Oser, J., Hooghe, M., & Marien, S. (2013). Is online participation distinct from offline participation? A latent class analysis of participation types and their stratification. *Political Research Quarterly*, 66(1), 91–101. https://doi.org/10.1177/1065912912436695

Paige, J. M. (1971). Political orientation and riot participation. *American Sociological Review*, 36(5), 810–820. https://doi.org/10.2307/2093668

Papacharissi, Z. (2004). Democracy online: Civility, politeness, and the democratic potential of online political discussion groups. *New Media & Society*, 6(2), 259–283.

Park, C. S. (2019). Learning politics from social media: Interconnection of social media use for political news and political issue and process knowledge. *Communication Studies*, 70(3), 253–276.

Park, C. S., & Kaye, B. K. (2018a). News engagement on social media and democratic citizenship: Direct and moderating roles of curatorial news use in political involvement. *Journalism and Mass Communication Quarterly*, 95(4), 1103–1127. https://doi.org/10.1177/1077699017753149

Park, C. S., & Kaye, B. K. (2018b). News engagement on social media and democratic citizenship: Direct and moderating roles of curatorial news use in political involvement. *Journalism and Mass Communication Quarterly*, 95(4), 1103–1127. https://doi.org/10.1177/1077699017753149

Park, C. S., & Kaye, B. K. (2019). Mediating roles of news curation and news elaboration in the relationship between social media use for news and political knowledge. *Journal of Broadcasting & Electronic Media*, 63(3), 455–473. https://doi.org/10.1080/08838151.2019.1653070

Parry, G., Moyser, G., & Day, N. (1992). Political participation and democracy in Britain. Cambridge University Press.

Parvin, P. (2018). Democracy without participation: A new politics for a disengaged era. *Res Publica*, 24(1), 31–52. https://doi.org/10.1007/s11158-017-9382-1

Pasek, J., more, eian, & Romer, D. (2009). Realizing the social internet? Online social networking meets offline civic engagement. *Journal of Information Technology & Politics*, 6(3/4), 197–215.

Pastrana Valls, A. (2017). The impact of cognitive mobility and the media on the political participation of mexicans. *Cuadernos Info*, 40, 17–37. https://doi.org/10.7764/cdi.40.1096

Pennebaker, J. W. (1997). Writing about emotional experiences as a therapeutic process. *Psychological Science*, 8(3), 162–166.

Penney, J. (2016). Motivations for participating in "viral politics": A qualitative case study of Twitter users and the 2012 US presidential election. *Convergence*, 22(1), 71–87. https://doi.org/10.1177/1354856514532074

Penney, J. (2017). Social media and citizen participation in "official" and "unofficial" electoral promotion: A structural analysis of the 2016 Bernie Sanders digital campaign. *Journal of Communication*, 67(3), 402–423. https://doi.org/10.1111/jcom.12300

Pew Research Center (2021). Social media fact sheet. Pew Research Center: Internet, Science & Tech. www.pewresearch.org/internet/fact-sheet/social-media/

Pillay, P. (2019). Online youth political engagement and bureaucratization: The Australian Youth Forum. *Convergence*, 25(4), 767–781. https://doi.org/10.1177/1354856517750363

Pingree, R. (2015). Effects of online political messages on their senders. In New technologies and civic engagement: New agendas in communication (ed. H. Gil De Zúñiga Navajas). New York: Routledge, 139–151.

Pingree, R. J. (2007). How messages affect their senders: A more general model of message effects and implications for deliberation. *Communication Theory*, 17(4), 439–461.

Plotke, D. (1997). Representation is democracy. *Constellations*, 4(1), 19–34. https://doi.org/10.1111/1467-8675.00033

Prensky, M. (2001). Digital natives, digital immigrants, part 2: Do they really think differently? *On the Horizon*, 9(6), 1–6. https://doi.org/10.1108/10748120110424843

Quandt, T., Frischlich, L., Boberg, S., & Schatto-Eckrodt, T. (2019). Fake news. In The international encyclopedia of journalism studies (eds. K. Meier, T. P. Vos, F. Hanusch, D. Dimitrakopoulou, M. Geertsema-Sligh & A. Sehl), pp. 1–6. Wiley: Hoboken, NJ. https://doi.org/10.1002/9781118841570.iejs0128

Rice, L. L., & Moffett, K. W. (2019). Snapchat and civic engagement among college students. *Journal of Information Technology and Politics*, 16(2), 87–104. https://doi.org/10.1080/19331681.2019.1574249

Ridge-Newman, A. (2020). Digital media as a driver of change in political organisation: 2010 and 2015 UK general elections. *Media, Culture & Society*, 42(7/8), 1343–1359.

Robles, J. M., Torres-Albero, C., Antino, M., & De Marco, S. (2015). The use of digital social networks from an analytical sociology perspective: The case of Spain. *Rationality and Society*, 27(4), 492–512. https://doi.org/10.1177/1043463115605480

Rojas, H., & Puig-i-Abril, E. (2009). Mobilizers mobilized: Information, expression, mobilization and participation in the digital age. *Journal of Computer-Mediated Communication*, 14(4), 902–927. https://doi.org/10.1111/j.1083-6101.2009.01475.x

Rosa, M. R. (2019). Verificado Mexico 2018: Disinformation and fact-checking on electoral campaign. *Revista de Comunicacion*, 18(1), 234–258. https://doi.org/10.26441/RC18.1-2019-A12

Rosema, M. (2007). Low turnout: Threat to democracy or blessing in disguise? Consequences of citizens' varying tendencies to vote. *Electoral Studies*, 26(2), 612–623. https://doi.org/10.1016/j.electstud.2006.10.007

Rosenstone, S., & Wolfinger, R. (1980). Who votes? Yale University Press: New Haven, CT.

Saldaña, M., Mcgregor, S. C., & Zúñiga, H. G. (2015). Social media as a public space for politics: Cross-national comparison of news consumption and participatory behaviors in the United States and the United Kingdom. *International Journal of Communication*, 9(1), 3304–3326.

Schaffner, B. F., & Streb, M. J. (2002). The partisan heuristic in low-information elections. *Public Opinion Quarterly*, 66(4), 559–581. https://doi.org/10.1086/343755

Scherman, A., Arriagada, A., & Valenzuela, S. (2015). Student and environmental protests in Chile: The role of social media. *Politics*, 35(2), 151–171. https://doi.org/10.1111/1467-9256.12072

Scheufele, D. A. (2000). Talk or conversation? Dimensions of interpersonal discussion and their implications for participatory democracy. *Journalism & Mass Communication Quarterly*, 77(4), 727–743.

Schlozman, K. L., Burns, N., & Verba, S. (1999). "What happened at work today?": A multistage model of gender, employment, and political participation. *The Journal of Politics*, 61(1), 29–53. https://doi.org/10.2307/2647774

Schlozman, K. L., Verba, S., & Brady, H. E. (2013). The unheavenly chorus: Unequal political voice and the broken promise of American democracy (Reprint edition). Princeton University Press: Princeton, NJ.

Shah, D. V. (2016). Conversation is the soul of democracy: Expression effects, communication mediation, and digital media. *Communication and the Public*, 1(1), 12–18. https://doi.org/10.1177/2057047316628310

Shah, D. V., Cho, J., Eveland Jr, W. P., & Kwak, N. (2005). Information and expression in a digital age: Modeling Internet effects on civic participation. *Communication Research*, 32(5), 531–565.

Shaw, T. C., Foster, K. A., & Combs, B. (2020). Disconnected in the Mecca? Black social media usage and levels of engagement in Atlanta. *Journal of Urban Affairs*, 44(6), 865–886. https://doi.org/10.1080/07352166.2020.1826326

Shehata, A., & Strömbäck, J. (2018). Learning political news from social media: Network media logic and current affairs news learning in a high-choice media environment. *Communication Research*, 1–23. https://doi.org/10.1177/0093650217749354

Sinpeng, A. (2021). Hashtag activism: Social media and the #FreeYouth protests in Thailand. *Critical Asian Studies*, 53(2), 192–205. https://doi.org/10.1080/14672715.2021.1882866

Skoric, M. M., & Poor, N. (2013). Youth engagement in Singapore: The interplay of social and traditional media. *Journal of Broadcasting & Electronic Media*, 57(2), 187–204. https://doi.org/10.1080/08838151.2013.787076

Skovsgaard, M., & Andersen, K. (2020). Conceptualizing news avoidance: Towards a shared understanding of different causes and potential solutions. *Journalism Studies*, 21(4), 459–476.

Soares, C. D. M., Joia, L. A., Altieri, D., & Lander Regasso, J. G. (2021). What's up? Mobile instant messaging apps and the truckers′ uprising in Brazil. *Technology in Society*, 64. https://doi.org/10.1016/j.techsoc.2020.101477

Somin, I. (2006). Knowledge about ignorance: New directions in the study of political information. *Critical Review*, 18(1–3), 255–278. https://doi.org/10.1080/08913810608443660

Somin, I. (2019). Rational ignorance and public choice. In The Oxford handbook of public choice, Volume 2 (eds. R. D. Congleton, B. N. Grofman & S. Voigt), pp. 571–587. Oxford University Press: New York. https://doi.org/10.1093/oxfordhb/9780190469771.013.29

Spaiser, V. (2012). Empowerment or democratic divide? Internet-based political participation of young immigrants and young natives in Germany. *Information Polity*, 17(2), 115–127. https://doi.org/10.3233/IP-2012-0268

Steinberg, A. (2015). Exploring Web 2.0 political engagement: Is new technology reducing the biases of political participation? *Electoral Studies*, 39, 102–116. https://doi.org/10.1016/j.electstud.2015.05.003

Strandberg, K. (2008). Public deliberation goes on-line? An analysis of citizens' political discussions on the internet prior to the finnish parliamentary elections in 2007. *Javnost: The Public*, 15(1), 71–89. https://doi.org/10.1080/13183222.2008.11008965

Strandberg, K. (2014). Mapping the online campaign audience: An analysis of online participation and its mobilizing potential in the 2011 Finnish parliamentary campaign. *Journal of Information Technology and Politics*, 11(3), 276–290. https://doi.org/10.1080/19331681.2014.895475

Stromback, J., Falasca, K., & Kruikemeier, S. (2018). The mix of media use matters: Investigating the effects of individual news repertoires on offline and online political participation. *Political Communication*, 35(3), 413–432. https://doi.org/10.1080/10584609.2017.1385549

Sylvester, D. E., & McGlynn, A. J. (2010). The digital divide, political participation, and place. *Social Science Computer Review*, 28(1), 64–74. https://doi.org/10.1177/0894439309335148

Tang, G., & Lee, F. L. F. (2013). Facebook use and political participation: The impact of exposure to shared political information, connections with public political actors, and network structural heterogeneity. *Social Science Computer Review*, 31(6), 763–773. https://doi.org/10.1177/0894439313490625

Theocharis, Y., & Lowe, W. (2016a). Does Facebook increase political participation? Evidence from a field experiment. *Information Communication and Society*, 19(10), 1465–1486. https://doi.org/10.1080/1369118X.2015.1119871

Towner, T. L. (2013). All political participation is socially networked? New media and the 2012 election. *Social Science Computer Review*, 31(5), 527–541. https://doi.org/10.1177/0894439313489656

Towner, T. L., & Muñoz, C. L. (2018). Baby boom or bust? The new media effect on political participation. *Journal of Political Marketing*, 17(1), 32–61. https://doi.org/10.1080/15377857.2016.1153561

Trenz, H.-J. (2009). Digital media and the return of the representative public sphere. *Javnost: the Public*, 16(1), 33–46.

Vaccari, C., & Valeriani, A. (2018a). Digital political talk and political participation: Comparing established and third wave democracies. *SAGE Open*, 8(2). https://doi.org/10.1177/2158244018784986

Vaccari, C., & Valeriani, A. (2018b). Dual screening, public service broadcasting, and political participation in eight Western democracies. *International Journal of Press/Politics*, 23(3), 367–388. https://doi.org/10.1177/1940161218779170

Valenzuela, S. (2013). Unpacking the use of social media for protest behavior: The roles of information, opinion expression, and activism. *American Behavioral Scientist*, 57(7), 920–942. https://doi.org/10.1177/0002764213479375

Valenzuela, S., Arriagada, A., & Scherman, A. (2014). Facebook, Twitter, and youth engagement: A quasi-experimental study of social media use and protest behavior using propensity score matching. *International Journal of Communication*, 8, 2046–2070.

Valenzuela, S., Bachmann, I., & Bargsted, M. (2019). The personal is the political? What do WhatsApp users share and how it matters for news knowledge, polarization and participation in Chile. *Digital Journalism*. https://doi.org/10.1080/21670811.2019.1693904

Valenzuela, S., Correa, T., & Zúñiga, H. (2018). Ties, likes, and tweets: Using strong and weak ties to explain differences in protest participation across Facebook and Twitter use. *Political Communication*, 35(1), 117–134. https://doi.org/10.1080/10584609.2017.1334726

Valenzuela, S., Kim, Y., & Gil de Zúñiga, H. (2012). Social networks that matter: Exploring the role of political discussion for online political participation. *International Journal of Public Opinion Research*, 24(2), 163–184. https://doi.org/10.1093/ijpor/edr037

Valeriani, A., & Vaccari, C. (2016). Accidental exposure to politics on social media as online participation equalizer in Germany, Italy, and the United Kingdom. *New Media & Society*, 18(9), 1857–1874. https://doi.org/10.1177/1461444815616223

Valkenburg, P. M. (2017). Understanding self-effects in social media. *Human Communication Research*, 43(4), 477–490.

Verba, S., Schlozman, K. L., & Brady, H. E. (1995). Voice and equality: Civic voluntarism in American politics. Harvard University Press: Cambridge, MA.

Vicente, M. R., & Novo, A. (2014). An empirical analysis of e-participation. The role of social networks and e-government over citizens' online engagement. *Government Information Quarterly*, 31(3), 379–387. https://doi.org/10.1016/j.giq.2013.12.006

Vissers, S., & Stolle, D. (2014a). Spill-over effects between Facebook and on/offline political participation? Evidence from a two-wave panel study. *Journal of Information Technology and Politics*, 11(3), 259–275. https://doi.org/10.1080/19331681.2014.888383

Vissers, S., & Stolle, D. (2014b). The internet and new modes of political participation: Online versus offline participation. *Information Communication and Society*, 17(8), 937–955. https://doi.org/10.1080/1369118X.2013.867356

Vochocová, L., Štětka, V., & Mazák, J. (2016). Good girls don't comment on politics? Gendered character of online political participation in the Czech Republic. *Information Communication and Society*, 19(10), 1321–1339. https://doi.org/10.1080/1369118X.2015.1088881

Wang, H., Cai, T., Mou, Y., & Shi, F. (2018). Traditional resources, internet resources, and youth online political participation: The resource theory revisited in the Chinese context. *Chinese Sociological Review*, 50(2), 115–136. https://doi.org/10.1080/21620555.2017.1341813

Wang, Y., McKee, M., Torbica, A., & Stuckler, D. (2019). Systematic literature review on the spread of health-related misinformation on social media. *Social Science & Medicine*, 240. https://doi.org/10.1016/j.socscimed.2019.112552

Wattenberg, M. (2020). Is voting for young people? Routledge: New York.

Weare, C. (2002). The internet and democracy: The causal links between technology and politics. *International Journal of Public Administration*, 25(5), 659–691. https://doi.org/10.1081/PAD-120003294

Weber, L. M., Loumakis, A., & Bergman, J. (2003). Who participates and why? An analysis of citizens on the internet and the mass public. *Social Science Computer Review*, 21(1), 26–42. https://doi.org/10.1177/0894439302238969

Weitz-Shapiro, R., & Winters, M. S. (2017). Can citizens discern? Information credibility, political sophistication, and the punishment of corruption in Brazil. *Journal of Politics*, 79(1), 60–74. https://doi.org/10.1086/687287

Wilkins, D. J., Livingstone, A. G., & Levine, M. (2019). Whose tweets? The rhetorical functions of social media use in developing the Black Lives Matter movement. *British Journal of Social Psychology*, 58(4), 786–805. https://doi.org/10.1111/bjso.12318

Williams, J. R. (2019). The use of online social networking sites to nurture and cultivate bonding social capital: A systematic review of the literature from 1997 to 2018. *New Media & Society*, 21(11–12), 2710–2729. https://doi.org/10.1177/1461444819858749

Wolfsfeld, G., Yarchi, M., & Samuel-Azran, T. (2016). Political information repertoires and political participation. *New Media & Society*, 18(9), 2096–2115. https://doi.org/10.1177/1461444815580413

Woo Yoo, S., & Gil de Zúñiga, H. (2014). Connecting blog, Twitter and Facebook use with gaps in knowledge and participation. *Communication & Society*, 27(4), 33–48. https://doi.org/10.15581/003.27.4.33-48

Xenos, M., Vromen, A., & Loader, B. D. (2014). The great equalizer? Patterns of social media use and youth political engagement in three advanced democracies. *Information Communication and Society*, 17(2), 151–167. https://doi.org/10.1080/1369118X.2013.871318

Xu, P., Ye, Y., & Zhang, M. (2018). Assessing political participation on the Internet in contemporary China. *Chinese Journal of Communication*, 11(3), 243–266. https://doi.org/10.1080/17544750.2018.1445119

Yamamoto, M., Nah, S., & Bae, S. Y. (2019). Social media prosumption and online political participation: An examination of online communication processes. *New Media & Society*. https://doi.org/10.1177/1461444819886295

Yang, H. C., & DeHart, J. L. (2016). Social media use and online political participation among college students during the US election 2012. *Social Media and Society*, 2(1), 1–18. https://doi.org/10.1177/2056305115623802

Yoo, S. W., & Gil de Zúñiga, H. (2019). The role of heterogeneous political discussion and partisanship on the effects of incidental news exposure online. *Journal of Information Technology & Politics*, 16(1), 1–16. https://doi.org/10.1080/19331681.2018.1561346

Yoo, S. W., Kim, J. W., & Gil de Zúñiga, H. (2017). Cognitive benefits for senders: Antecedents and effects of political expression on social media. *Journalism & Mass Communication Quarterly*, 94(1), 17–37.

Yuan, C., & Yang, H. (2019). Research on k-value selection method of k-means clustering algorithm. *J*, 2(2), 226–235. https://doi.org/10.3390/j2020016

Zhang, N., & Skoric, M. M. (2018). Media use and environmental engagement: Examining differential gains from news media and social media. *International Journal of Communication*, 12, 380–403.

Zhang, W., Johnson, T. J., Seltzer, T., & Bichard, S. L. (2010). The revolution will be networked: The influence of social networking sites on political attitudes and behavior. *Social Science Computer Review*, 28(1), 75–92. https://doi.org/10.1177/0894439309335162

Zhang, W., Seltzer, T., & Bichard, S. L. (2013). Two sides of the coin: Assessing the influence of social network site use during the 2012 U.S. presidential campaign. *Social Science Computer Review*, 31(5), 542–551. https://doi.org/10.1177/0894439313489962

Zhang, X., & Lin, W. (2014). Political participation in an unlikely place: How individuals engage in politics through social networking sites in China. *International Journal of Communication*, 8(1), 21–42.

Zumarraga-Espinosa, M. (2020). Social network sites and political protest: An analysis of the moderating role of socioeconomic status and political group membership. *Doxa Comunicacion*, 30, 55–77. https://doi.org/10.31921/doxacom.n30a3

Funding Statement

The authors wish to acknowledge funding from the Spanish National Research Agency's Program for the Generation of Knowledge and the Scientific and Technological Strengthening Research and Development (PID2020-115562GB-I00)

Cambridge Elements ☰

Politics and Communication

Stuart Soroka

University of California

Stuart Soroka is a Professor in the Department of Communication at the University of California, Los Angeles, and Adjunct Research Professor at the Center for Political Studies at the Institute for Social Research, University of Michigan. His research focuses on political communication, political psychology, and the relationships between public policy, public opinion, and mass media. His books with Cambridge University Press include The Increasing Viability of Good News (2021, with Yanna Krupnikov), Negativity in Democratic Politics (2014), Information and Democracy (forthcoming, with Christopher Wlezien) and Degrees of Democracy (2010, with Christopher Wlezien).

About the Series

Cambridge Elements in Politics and Communication publishes research focused on the intersection of media, technology, and politics. The series emphasizes forward-looking reviews of the field, path-breaking theoretical and methodological innovations, and the timely application of social-scientific theory and methods to current developments in politics and communication around the world.

Cambridge Elements

Politics and Communication

Elements in the Series

A full series listing is available at: www.cambridge.org/EPCM

Printed in the United States
by Baker & Taylor Publisher Services